PLUNDER!

Taking Back the Treasures Hidden in Darkness

GARY KEESEE

TABLE OF CONTENTS

FOREWORD

This book was written with the intent to encourage you to face the impossible and allow God to challenge you past your comfort level and lead you into your destiny. But in order to get there, you need to see things you have never seen before and think thoughts you have never thought before.

The title of this book, I am sure, sounds a little strange. Let's face it, no one really uses the word "plunder" much anymore except God, who used it over and over again in the Bible. What that word implies will open a completely new understanding of the Kingdom and will make a dramatic impact on your finances.

To completely understand what it means to plunder, we must go back to a book I wrote several years ago called *Your Financial Revolution: The Power of Rest*. You could say, in a way, that this book is an extension of that book, picking up where it left off. That is why I am spending the first three chapters of this book reviewing what I taught in *Your Financial Revolution: The Power of Rest*. I really do not think you can understand what it means to plunder if you do not understand what was described in that book. But if you feel that you do understand what that book teaches, you may skip ahead to chapter four, but I would **strongly suggest** that you read the first three chapters of this book as a review.

Why this book? Why now? The Lord speaks to me every New Year's Eve about the coming year or about the coming decade. It has been that way for the last thirty years. But this year was different. Yes, He did speak to me on New Year's Eve, but He also spoke to me in early December about 2025 and beyond. He told me that He wanted me to start teaching what He was showing me before the new year began so that people could start thinking ahead. He wanted His people to be prepared for what was going to begin happening in 2025. To give you a quick summary of what He said: He told me there was going to be **a time of great harvest and plunder coming to the body of Christ**. Of course I had never used that word before and really did not know what it meant. So, I looked it up.

Plunder: something taken by force, theft, or fraud, often referring to the spoils of war or conquest.[1] I know that sounds like something we should stay away from, right? But not if you are taking back what the enemy has stolen!

I believe this word "plunder" is going to take on a completely new meaning in your life. In fact, I am sure it will totally change your understanding of our stand against Satan and his army of demons who want to steal every blessing of God from your life. But it is not too late to take back what the enemy has stolen! It is time to *Plunder*!

Gary Keesee

---

[1] "Plunder," Merriam-Webster dictionary, https://www.merriam-webster.com/dictionary/plunder.

CHAPTER 1

THERE IS MORE TO LIFE THAN PAYING THE BILLS!

At first, it seemed like a brief oasis from the extreme financial stress that seemed to overpower every day of our lives. We had invited about 50 people over to our old farmhouse for an afternoon to enjoy a bonfire, hot dogs, and fellowship. I was looking forward to the event as I was emotionally tired and needed something positive to focus on.

The evening was a great success. The food was great, many of our friends came with their children, and all were having a good time. The house was packed when there was a knock at the door. I thought it might be a latecomer to our meeting, but as I opened the door, I was greeted by an employee from the electric company. He politely said he was there to turn my power off for the unpaid bill.

I was horrified. My house was full of guests, and I needed the power to be on, besides the embarrassment that it would cause. I quickly asked the employee to step away from the house to the backyard for a minute. I asked him what it would take to keep the lights on, and he gave me an amount. "Too high," I thought. "Can you make it a bit lower?" He thought for a minute and finally gave me a lower number. "Can you hold the check until Tuesday before you deposit it?" I asked. He said, "No problem." So, I wrote out the check.

There was no money in the account that Friday, and I did not know how any would be there before Tuesday, but at least the power stayed on throughout the weekend. I do not remember what I did on Tuesday, but I probably found something to pawn in order to pay the bill.

This was one day in our life of living in financial dysfunction. Now, envision living that way for nine years! We did, and there is no joy in poverty! Living with IRS liens, judgments, ten maxed-out credit cards, three loans at over 29% interest—all late or in collections. Pawn shops were a way of life. Borrowing money from friends and family, totaling over $20,000, was an embarrassment. Driving two broken down cars that barely started added stress upon stress.

The turmoil of all the financial dysfunction and shame brought on panic attacks and antidepressants, which did not help. We lived in an old 1852 farmhouse with cracked windows held together by duct tape. The carpet we had found alongside the road; the appliances were bought at garage sales.

Living under that kind of stress stops all vision and siphons off every ounce of joy a day may bring. Every thought is focused on surviving; where to find the money for the next bill. Did I spend too much last week? Should I take my calculator grocery shopping with me to make sure I do not go over? Always thinking how to do something the cheapest way possible.

Friend, that is not living! No, it is hell on earth, a slow death that takes your life like a cancer, slowly stealing your strength and every dream you had ever hoped for. To make it through one more week was now the dream. Debt became a way of life, and slowly the noose tightened until there was no hope at all.

Nine years! Nine years of watching that noose tighten. Nine years of watching my kids go without the clothes they needed or wanted. Nine years that my wife had to put up with whatever she could find. I thought we were an anomaly, that everyone else was doing great. But I found out that behind the shiny new cars and beautiful homes, there is trouble. Here are a few of the stats I found for the year 2024.

- 33% of people experience extreme stress.[1]
- 77% of people experience stress that affects their physical health.[2]

---

[1] "Everything You Need to Know About Stress," Posted November 20, 2023, Mass General Brigham McLean, https://www.mcleanhospital.org/essential/stress.

[2] "Everything You Need to Know About Stress."

- 73% of people experience stress that impacts their mental health.[3]
- 48% of people report having sleep problems as a result of stress.[4]
- 74% of people have felt so stressed that they have been overwhelmed or unable to cope with it.[5]
- Nearly 70% of Americans experience physical and mental symptoms of stress.[6]

Everyone is running as hard as they can but getting nowhere.

A 2023 survey conducted by Payroll.org highlighted that 78% of Americans live paycheck to paycheck, a 6% increase from the previous year. In other words, more than three-quarters of Americans struggle to save or invest after paying for their monthly expenses.[7]

Drenda and I eventually ended up having no money, and no food in the house for our three children. We had already borrowed from anyone and everyone that would listen. Even our families cut us off.

---

[3] "Everything You Need to Know About Stress."

[4] "Everything You Need to Know About Stress."

[5] "Stress: Statistics," Mental Health Foundation, https://www.mentalhealth.org.uk/explore-mental-health/statistics/stress-statistics.

[6] "Stress Fact Sheet 2020," Mental Health Association of Maryland, https://www.mhamd.org/wp-content/uploads/2019/10/Stress-Fact-Sheet-2020.pdf.

[7] Batdorf, Emily, "Living Paycheck to Paycheck Statistics 2024," Posted April 2, 2024, *Forbes*, https://www.forbes.com/advisor/banking/living-paycheck-to-paycheck-statistics-2024/.

That is when I knew that I did not have the answer. I had worked hard, hoping that the next week in sales would be better, but it wasn't. Although Drenda and I were Christians and knew that God said He would provide for us, I never could seem to get heaven to show up.

I hit bottom when a phone call came—one of many—that demanded that I pay an outstanding debt, or they would file a lawsuit against me. However, I did not have any money to pay toward that debt, and I knew that I was done. In desperation, I made it upstairs to our bedroom and cried out to God. Suddenly, I heard His voice. In essence, He said that I was in this mess because I had never learned how His Kingdom worked. To be honest, I had no idea what He was talking about, but I know I heard the Lord. When I looked in the Bible, I saw that it said the same thing.

> *And do not set your heart on what you will eat or drink; do not worry about it. For the pagan world runs after all such things, and your Father knows that you need them. But seek his kingdom, and these things will be given to you as well.*
>
> —Luke 12:29–31 (NIV)

Seek the Kingdom, learn how the Kingdom works, and everything will be added to you. Wow! So that is what we did. We began to study the Kingdom of God with interest and began to learn that the Kingdom of God is a government with a King and laws.

Once I learned that I was a citizen of that great Kingdom (see Ephesians 2:19), I realized that I had legal rights and benefits in that Kingdom. As God began to teach us those laws, we began to apply them, and amazingly, God showed us how to reorganize our company in a dream one night.

By making those changes and continuing to learn about the Kingdom, we became debt free in about two and a half years. We then went on to create more businesses, and soon we were able to give hundreds of thousands away toward ministry projects. We were able to build our dream home and pay for it. Our life drastically changed! It was really like a dream, and we had to pinch ourselves almost every day as we watched the Kingdom of God manifest before our eyes!

(If you want to learn the full story of what God taught us, please check out my five-book series titled *Your Financial Revolution* at Amazon or Faithlifenow.com.)

> *"Therefore I tell you, do not worry about your life, what you will eat or drink; or about your body, what you will wear. <u>Is not life more than food, and the body more than clothes</u>?"*
> —Matthew 6:25 (NIV)

Do not worry? Worry and fear had been a constant companion before we learned how the Kingdom worked. We had life flipped upside down. We were running after things and success instead of running after God. As we made those changes and learned how the Kingdom worked, guess what—**IT WORKED**, just like the Bible said it would.

In the above verse, Jesus is saying that the things of life are not in themselves life! Since the day that Adam and Eve rebelled against God in the garden of Eden, life flipped upside down and now everything that supports life is more important than life itself.

People have no clue what real life is, and they certainly do not know who they really are. Ask anyone who they are, and they will tell you what they do: I am a doctor, I am a realtor, etc. No, that is not who you are, it is what you do.

Man has lost his dreams. What I mean is that man now dreams of how to make more money but has lost the dream of purpose. In other words, whatever is paying the most money becomes his dream. However, because each person is uniquely created with different talents and abilities, they find themselves in an occupation or job that is not their passion. Life then endures long, drawn-out weeks waiting for freedom on the weekend, or long, drawn-out lives waiting to retire.

So, let me ask you a question. If you had no need for money, had more money than you could ever spend in your lifetime, what would you do? You would probably come up with something different than what you are doing right now. I know from statistics that at least 70% of Americans when asked if they like their job, said they are not doing what they love.[8] I want you to understand that this running after wealth, this pressure to perform, and the constant worry over tomorrow, was never the plan of God in the beginning.

> *So God created mankind in his own image, in the image of God he created them; male and female he created them. God blessed them and said to them, "Be fruitful and increase in number; fill the earth and subdue it. Rule over the fish in the sea and the birds in the sky and over every living creature that moves on the ground."*
>
> *Then God said, "I give you every seed-bearing plant on the face of the whole earth and every tree that has fruit with seed in it. They will be yours for food. And to all the beasts of the earth and all the birds in the sky and all the creatures that move along the ground—everything that has the breath of life in it—I give every green plant for food." And it was so. God saw all that he had made, and it was very good. And there was evening, and there was morning—the sixth day.*
>
> —Genesis 1:27–31 (NIV)

---

[8] Sturt, David, and Todd Nordstrom, "10 Shocking Workplace Stats You Need To Know," Posted March 8, 2018, *Forbes*, https://www.forbes.com/sites/davidsturt/2018/03/08/10-shocking-workplace-stats-you-need-to-know/?sh=3130ab42f3af.

Man was created on the sixth day of creation, at the end of the sixth day, to be exact. He was created at the end of the sixth day because he was created to dwell with God on the seventh day, the day we know as the day of rest, where everything was prepared for man to live here on the earth.

THE CONSTANT WORRY OVER TOMORROW WAS NEVER THE PLAN OF GOD IN THE BEGINNING.

But rest is far from how most people live today. Most of the families living paycheck to paycheck would laugh at you. Rest? Most of them are working two or even three jobs just to survive. Most have given up on their dreams, and simply look forward to the weekend to find a little time to stop before they go back to work on Monday. Paying the bills and going to work is what most people know. Dreams? Who can afford those?

Before Adam and Eve rebelled against God, they had no worries. Everything they needed, God supplied.

> *Thus the heavens and the earth were <u>completed</u> in all their vast array.*
>
> *By the seventh day God had <u>finished</u> the work he had been doing; so on the seventh day he rested from all his work. Then God blessed the seventh day and made it holy, because on it he rested from all the work of creating that he had done.*
> —Genesis 2:1–3 (NIV)

The Bible says that God rested on the seventh day. He was not tired! He was finished. Everything was complete. Everything that man would ever have need of was already on the earth when man showed up. Peace!

Man had all the provision he would ever need; there was no worry about paying the bills, no worrying over being sick. He had a perfect body and a perfect wife. The only thing they would focus on was each other, God, and their assignment or purpose. Adam was in charge of the earth; he ruled over it completely by the authority and power that God had given him on behalf of the Kingdom of God.

But we already know how that story ended. Adam and Eve committed treason against the Kingdom of God and lost their position, lost their provision, and lost their purpose. Their purpose now became survival. Worry and fear now consumed their thoughts, and the struggle to survive, as Genesis 3:17 says, would now require painful toil and sweat.

> *To Adam he said, "Because you listened to your wife and ate fruit from the tree about which I commanded you, 'You must not eat from it,'*
>
> *"Cursed is the ground because of you;*
> *through **painful toil** you will eat food from it*
> *all the days of your life.*
> *It will produce thorns and thistles for you,*
> *and you will eat the plants of the field.*

*By the **sweat** of your brow*
  you will eat your food
until you return to the ground,
  since from it you were taken;
for dust you are
  and to dust you will return."

—Genesis 3:17–19 (NIV)

Adam lost the seventh day!

There was now no rest, there was no peace, and there was no provision. Instead of a lush garden full of all the food they could ever want, there were now only thorns and thistles. Only by painful toil and sweat would the earth provide the provision that Adam needed or wanted. In the frenzy to survive, Adam lost sight of his purpose, which originally was to rule over the earth on behalf of the Kingdom of God. Now his purpose shifted to survival. He was forced to run (labor) with painful toil and sweat after his provision.

A darkness enveloped his life and Adam had to run to stay ahead of the void. Man has lived in this state of darkness ever since. But there was and is hope. When man fell, God gave him a remembrance, a picture if you will, of what he would someday restore to His creation; this picture was called the Sabbath day.

The word Sabbath literally means "rest." The seventh day of the week was given to man as a Sabbath day. The requirement for the Sabbath day, as you can imagine, was to do no work, no sweating and painful toil was allowed. It was a day when man was to stop, enjoy his family, and worship God. All the provisions for the Sabbath had to be completed before the Sabbath began. Even the Sabbath meal had to be prepared the night before. It was a day of rest with full provision and every detail of possible need already attended to. Man could stop and think of something other than survival.

The Sabbath day was just that: a day. But man has been dreaming of a life of rest ever since. Man's quest for wealth is a symptom of his desire to be free from the painful toil and sweat curse that has held him prisoner his entire life. Wealth lures us with the possible escape to a place of rest. A place where we can focus on what we really want to do—a life full of purpose instead of survival.

Today the Sabbath, the seventh day, whether you celebrate it on Saturday or Sunday, is not held in high honor in our culture. Yes, most people that do attend church do go on Sunday morning, yet looking at the culture as a whole, you would not be able to tell it apart from any other workday.

When I was a child, everything was closed on Sunday. You could not go shopping on Sunday. You could not even buy gas on Sunday. My father would have to buy gas on Saturday nights to be sure he had what he needed on Sunday.

If you know much about me, you know I enjoy hunting, but as a hunter, I could not even hunt on Sunday. It was illegal to hunt on Sunday. People used to wear their finest clothes and have big family dinners on Sunday. But of course, that has all changed.

But no matter how well the Sabbath was prepared for, no matter how great the family meal, Monday was coming. The term "Monday morning blues" has been synonymous with the word "dread" for as long as I can remember. "I have to go to work" and "back to the old grindstone" were phrases that were used to describe Monday morning, and if you stop and think about it, it almost sounded like slavery. But thank God, it's Friday! Even today, the weekend and the Sabbath do offer a brief resting place for most people. But it is short-lived, and the Monday morning traffic jam awaits.

But what if there really was a way to escape the earth curse system of just surviving. How awesome it would be if there really was a way to live life free from fear, full of provision, full of purpose, and living in a place of rest! Drenda and I lived a life of torment, fear, sickness and insecurity for nine long years until we found that the Sabbath rest was in fact an option for our lives. I am serious!

> *There remains, then, a Sabbath-rest for the people of God; for anyone who enters God's rest also rests from their works, just as God did from his. Let us, therefore, make every effort to enter*

> *that rest, so that no one will perish by following*
> *their example of disobedience.*
> —Hebrews 4:9–11 (NIV)

Friend, please take a moment to read over that Scripture one more time. At first glance, I am sure you immediately might dismiss it, thinking it has to do with the Old Testament. But, no, this is a New Testament promise to the church. There is a Sabbath rest available for the people of God today.

This Scripture implies that we can enter into God's rest, with everything complete and provided for us to live our lives outside the earth curse system. There is freedom from the survival mentality, freedom from being imprisoned by poverty, and freedom from sickness and disease. There are new options!

Again, let me emphasize that the Sabbath rest was not just Old Testament information; it is for you today as well. But before you think I am talking about living under all the Old Testament legalism and rituals again, I am not. Instead, I want to examine this Sabbath rest that Hebrews talks about. Because as Drenda and I have found out, understanding this truth is a vital key to having the provision you need.

SHOCKER: THE SABBATH IS NOT A DAY ANY LONGER!

I hope that statement got your attention. There has been great discussion in the body of Christ stating how the

Sabbath should be celebrated: Saturday, Sunday, or beginning at sundown on Friday night until sundown on Saturday evening. Whole denominations have been built around their interpretation of the Sabbath. Before you throw this book across the room in disgust, thinking I am a heretic, please bear with me for just a moment and let's take a look at Colossians 2:16–17.

> *Therefore do not let anyone judge you by what you eat or drink, or with regard to a religious festival, a New Moon celebration or a Sabbath day. These are a shadow of the things that were to come; the reality, however, is found in Christ.*
> —Colossians 2:16–17 (NIV)

Pay close attention to what Paul says: the Sabbath day was a shadow of the things that were to come; **the reality, however, is found in Christ.** The Sabbath day was a shadow; it was not the real thing. If Christ is the real thing, then the Sabbath day was a shadow of who He is and what He did.

Let me say it this way. There is no power in the Sabbath day to take or change the earth curse system of painful toil and sweat that Adam brought into the earth realm. If you religiously honor it, by itself and of itself, it has no power to set you free. But it is a shadow, a picture, of what you will find in Christ. Let me say this: the Sabbath is not a day, it is a person, who is Jesus. He is our Sabbath and He has restored to us everything the Sabbath was showing us.

When I was in first grade, my teacher had all of us make silhouette drawings of our head from the side. They took a projector and had us sit in front of it, casting a shadow of our head onto a white piece of paper. They then drew the outline of our shadow and created our silhouette, which we cut out and took home to our mothers for Mother's Day. The shadow did capture some likeness of me, but it did not capture my essence, my character or personality. But it did give some information about me.

The Sabbath did the same thing. Its shadow, its picture, pointed to Christ which indicated that this new covenant Jesus was putting in place would give us back the ability to prosper and have the provision we needed to escape the earth curse system. It reestablished us as sons and daughters of God and citizens of God's great Kingdom! Again, the Sabbath was a picture of what Jesus would someday bring back to us.

Let me give you another example. If I showed you a picture of a plate full of chocolate chip cookies and a glass of milk, you would probably say that looked really good. But if I actually gave you a plate of cookies with milk, and you were able to enjoy the real thing, you would say the real thing is much better than the picture.

This is what Colossians is showing us. The Sabbath was simply a picture of life without the painful toil and sweat curse. But Colossians tells us that Jesus is actually the reality of that picture, the real thing. And since we are in Christ, we have that reality! I know what you are thinking: that cannot be true, but it is. I am not saying that our goal is to just sit around and drink iced tea all day. No, there will be labor in the new reality Jesus is giving us, but that will be labor to gather in the harvest, an abundant and overflowing harvest!

Let me give you an example. Let's say that I was digging a ditch in my backyard and I hit gold gravel, pure 24-karat gold stones. But gold is not light stuff, and I was getting tired of digging. So, I walk over to your house and show you the pile of gold that I have dug out and tell you that every shovel I pull out is full of these gold stones, but I am getting tired and thought I needed to take a ten-minute break to rest. So, I thought that you, being my neighbor, might like to dig for a bit as I take that break.

So, let me ask you, how long of a coffee break are you going to take? This is my point. People love to labor around their dreams. They love to labor in the harvest season. Again, I am not saying we will not need to labor when Jesus ushers us into Sabbath rest. But what I am saying is that the labor that we want to do will be meaningful and a pleasure to do.

Unfortunately for most people, they do not really understand the Sabbath. The Sabbath for most people today is a religious day. People look upon the Sabbath as God's day, a day where we owe it to God to go to church, do stuff for God, and do other religious things. Jesus had to correct his disciples who had the same mindset,

> ***"The Sabbath was made for man, not man for the Sabbath."***
>
> —Mark 2:27b (NIV)

The Sabbath was made for man, not man for the Sabbath. Did you know that a lot of people feel guilty if they miss church? Why would they feel guilty for missing church when in fact they are the church? I am not saying we should not assemble together in worship at all, but that mindset indicates that they have a wrong view of the Sabbath.

Let me be clear, there is a supernatural rest available to you. I am not talking about sleeping or taking a break, I am talking about having everything you need, your life being complete with no fear and having overflowing provision.

> *"Give, and it will be given to you. A good measure, pressed down, shaken together and **running over**, will be poured into your lap. For with the measure you use, it will be measured to you."*
>
> —Luke 6:38 (NIV)

Look at Deuteronomy 28, and what it says about your legal inheritance. Although this was spoken to Israel as the blessing of Abraham, meaning Abraham and all his descendants. We Gentiles were grafted into that blessing.

> *He redeemed us in order that the **blessing given to Abraham might come to the Gentiles through Christ Jesus,** so that by faith we might receive the promise of the Spirit.*
> —Galatians 3:14 (NIV)

The blessing given to Abraham was these promises, recorded in Deuteronomy 28. They are now your promises as well!

> *The Lord will send a blessing on your barns and on everything you put your hand to. The Lord your God will bless you in the land he is giving you.*
>
> *The Lord will establish you as his holy people, as he promised you on oath, if you keep the commands of the Lord your God and walk in obedience to him. Then all the peoples on earth will see that you are called by the name of the Lord, and they will fear you. The Lord will grant you abundant prosperity— in the fruit of your womb, the young of your livestock and the crops of your ground—in the land he swore to your ancestors to give you.*

The Lord will open the heavens, the storehouse of
his bounty, to send rain on your land in season
and to bless all the work of your hands. You will
lend to many nations but will borrow from none.
The Lord will make you the head, not the tail.

—Deuteronomy 28: 8–13a (NIV)

If you are going to lend to nations, or if you are going to lend at all, you must have some money to lend. God wants to bless you abundantly!

Before I go further, let's not lose sight of our promise here in Hebrews.

There remains, then, a Sabbath-rest for the
people of God; for anyone who enters God's rest
also rests from their works, just as God did from
his.

—Hebrews 4:9–10 (NIV)

The shadow of the Sabbath day says you do not need to toil and sweat for what you need on the Sabbath day. It was actually forbidden that you do any labor on the Sabbath. But let's remember the Sabbath was only giving us a glimpse, a picture, of what Jesus restored to us when He gave us the new covenant.

The new covenant that He put in place would free us from the earth curse system of having to toil and sweat just to survive and would allow God to bless us abundantly. In other words, what the Sabbath day showed us in its picture became a reality in Christ. So, what is the picture telling you?

CHAPTER 2

WAIT, THERE'S MORE!

There remains, then, a Sabbath-rest for the people
of God; for anyone who enters God's rest also rests
from their works, just as God did from his.
(Hebrews 4:9–10, NIV)

We have already confirmed that this Scripture is telling us, the New Testament believer, that the Sabbath rest is for us today and has not passed away. We also have pointed out that the Sabbath was only a picture of what Jesus would someday restore. The fact that they could not work on the Sabbath said that we would be freed from the painful toil and sweat of the earth curse system of survival.

Therefore do not let anyone judge you by what you
eat or drink, or with regard to a religious festival, a
New Moon celebration or a Sabbath day. These
*are a shadow of the things that were to come; **the***
reality, however, is found in Christ.
—Colossians 2:16–17 (NIV)

The shadow of the Sabbath day says you could not toil and sweat for what you needed on the Sabbath day. That picture was looking forward, showing us a glimpse of what Jesus would do when He came, which was freeing us from the earth curse system of having to toil and sweat to survive.

In other words, what the picture showed us has now become a reality in Christ. The earth curse held men and women captive to a system that required them to run after provision. Because of this, men and women often found themselves having to make tough decisions regarding their survival requiring them to abandon their dreams and passions that God gave them, just to "make a living."

When Jesus triumphed over Satan and destroyed his hold on mankind, God was then able to bless those who called on the name of Jesus with the anointing and ability to prosper above the earth curse. I say it this way: until you fix the money thing, you will never find your God-designed destiny.

Restoring heaven's ability to bless you as God wanted to is reflected in Jesus's first message that He ever preached.

> *Jesus returned to Galilee in the power of the Spirit, and news about him spread through the whole countryside. He was teaching in their synagogues, and everyone praised him.*
>
> *He went to Nazareth, where he had been brought up, and on the Sabbath day he went into the synagogue, as was his custom. He stood up to read, and the scroll of the prophet Isaiah was handed to him. Unrolling it, he found the place where it is written:*
>
> *"The Spirit of the Lord is on me, because he has anointed me to proclaim good news to the poor. He has sent me to proclaim freedom for the prisoners*

and recovery of sight for the blind,
to set the oppressed free,
to proclaim the year of the Lord's favor."

—Luke 4:14–19 (NIV)

This is the first message preached!

By saying that there was a way out of poverty, He was saying there was a way out of the earth curse system of painful toil and sweat. It was this slavery, running after provision, that held men prisoners, unable to find rest.

But the Sabbath Day was not the only picture that God gave His people of what was someday going to be restored. There was also the Sabbath year!

At the end of every seven years you must cancel debts. This is how it is to be done: Every creditor shall cancel any loan they have made to a fellow Israelite. They shall not require payment from anyone among their own people, because the Lord's time for canceling debts has been proclaimed. You may require payment from a foreigner, but you must cancel any debt your fellow Israelite owes you. However, there need be no poor people among you, for in the land the Lord your God is giving you to possess as your inheritance, he will richly bless you, if only you fully obey the Lord your God and are careful to follow all these commands I am giving you today. For the Lord your God will bless you as he has promised, and you will lend to many nations but will borrow from none. You will rule over many nations but none will rule over you.

—Deuteronomy 15:1–6 (NIV)

Notice that they were to cancel all debts every seven years. Again, we see God using the number seven to show that everything is complete, there is no lack, and He has provided everything needed for man.

Yet it is possible and probable that some upon hearing this might question God's wisdom in this. After all, if someone owes you money, you would probably want to be paid. But God answers them this way, "*However, there should be no poor among you, for in the land the Lord your God is giving you to possess as your inheritance, he will richly bless you.*" (Deuteronomy 15:4, NIV)

DEBT IS A SYSTEM BASED ON INSUFFICIENCY, BUT GOD IS GOING TO COMPLETELY PROVIDE FOR YOU AND DEBT WILL NO LONGER BE NEEDED IN YOUR LIFE

He goes on to say that they would be so blessed that they would become the lenders and not the borrowers, the head and not the tail. Who would not sign up for that? Again, I want to remind you that this is talking about the benefit of the Sabbath year, which, if you remember, is a shadow of what you have now as a modern-day Christian.

As on the Sabbath day, they were not to painfully toil and sweat, thus they were not allowed to sow their crops—for a whole year!

At this point, someone may say, "Hey, I can survive one day with what is in the fridge but surviving a whole year without working is a little more difficult."

So here again, the shadow, the picture, is pointing forward to Jesus and what He will restore to us. What is the picture telling you? Simply that debt will not be needed any longer, because God is going to bless you! Debt is a system based on insufficiency, but God is going to completely provide for you and debt will no longer be needed in your life. God is not saying that you cannot use debt, He is saying that you will no longer need to lean to debt, trust in, or rely on debt to survive.

If this is true then I think you can agree with Jesus's words, that He came to preach good news to the poor!

But wait! There is more: the biggest picture yet to show God's people what was to come. It was called the Year of Jubilee.

What you are about to read is amazing—no, let me rephrase that—you will actually think it is totally impossible and too good to be true. I am talking about the Year of Jubilee: the greatest picture of what Jesus restored to you in your finances. Yet few people even know or understand that they have this.

We have already talked about the Sabbath day and the Sabbath year, both of which are shadows of what we have in Christ, but now we come to the big event, the Year of Jubilee.

Just the name sounds like a celebration, doesn't it? However, in the realm of finances, most people, and sadly most Christians, do not have much to celebrate.

As you may know, I have been active in the financial field for 43 years now, owning multiple companies during that time and working with tens, if not hundreds, of thousands of people with their personal finances during that same time. So, I know what is out there. And I know what is usually behind the shiny new car or the nice big home, usually a lot of debt and stress.

Hey, I am not knocking having a nice car or a big home; it just costs a lot of money today to live, and unfortunately most people go into slavery to accomplish it. The earth curse system is a survival system that is usually going to fall short of setting people free. Trust me, of all the thousands and thousands of people I have met, most were not bad people; they were doing the best they could on their own and they did not know of God's Kingdom or what I am sharing in this book.

Of course, you know that Drenda and I lived in financial slavery for nine long, hard years ourselves until we learned about the Sabbath rest and how the Kingdom operates. After living that way for so long, you do not realize how much dysfunction you put up with and think is normal.

As I said earlier, by studying the Kingdom of God and learning and applying the laws of the Kingdom to our finances, we became debt free and began to prosper at a level that I had never experienced. We were able to give thousands, then hundreds of thousands, away to ministry projects as we continued to increase. Drenda and I had to pinch ourselves over and over again as we watched the Kingdom of God function before our eyes.

As we continued to prosper, with no debt and plenty of money in the bank, I found that we began to get a little content. Although we were doing great, God began to deal with me about my small thinking. Small thinking? I thought I was doing pretty good. Yes, I was out of debt. Yes, I had seen some amazing things happen. And yes, I was happy and content. But I had stopped dreaming, and God knew it, and He wanted me to stretch again. There was more territory to take, and more projects to fund. I had gotten a little stale. Happy, but stale.

As I said, I own a financial services company, and I am invited every year by one of my vendors to an event to celebrate the previous year's success. The attendance is usually around 250 of the top associates and executives in the company. It is an all-expense paid trip to some really great places, but for the top few, there would be special recognition and $100,000 bonus checks.

Because I was busy pastoring a large church, doing TV, and running my company, I always felt that I just did not have time to do the production needed to reach the upper recognition level. But this particular year, as I sat in the meeting and watched the top 10 associates get recognized and receive their bonus checks, I was convicted. I heard God's voice, "I want you up there. I want My glory seen here."

Wait a minute; how could I do that? I am already maxed out pastoring the church, homeschooling the kids with Drenda, and running the company at the level it is producing. But since God said I should be up there, He must know how I could do it.

So Drenda and I made up our minds right then and there that we would be up on that stage the next year. But how? We had no idea. For the past 10 years I had been doing about 3 to 4 million a year with this vendor, but the production required to achieve the top 10 would be around 10 million. I had no idea how I was going to reach that level, and not even sure it was possible with my schedule. And besides that, it was already March. The year was already well under way and I was nowhere close to being on pace to reach that goal.

One thing I had learned though was, if that goal was possible, I could not get it done in my own strength. So Drenda and I prayed and set our goal, sowing a financial seed and releasing our faith for the ten million in production needed to qualify. Once we sowed our seed, we called it done and began thanking God for it.

To make a long story short, God showed me how to reach my goal in a dream. He showed me exactly what I needed to do, and as long as I did what He had shown me, I would reach it.

Do you know that we made that ten-million-dollar goal that year by one sale! What a thrill to be up on that stage at the next convention with the top ten in the company and receive that $100,000 bonus.

Do you want to know how great that felt? It was just a huge party. Not only had we reached our goal and received the bonus check, but our income had also climbed by hundreds of thousands of dollars that year as well. Since that year, we have consistently been in the top tier with that vendor and have been receiving those bonus checks and enjoying sharing the goodness of God with many who attend those events. Sounds like a party to me!

So, when I start talking about some Old Testament event like the Year of Jubilee, don't nod off and think this is boring stuff, because it is not. Remember, life goes better with a party, so let's take a look at the biggest event/party that Israel celebrated and learn how to have your own.

The Year of Jubilee

"'Count off seven Sabbath years—seven times seven years—so that the seven Sabbath years amount to a period of forty-nine years. Then have the trumpet sounded everywhere on the tenth day of the seventh month; on the Day of Atonement sound the trumpet throughout your land. Consecrate the fiftieth year and proclaim liberty throughout the land to all its inhabitants. It shall be a jubilee for you; each of you is to return to your family property and to your own clan. The fiftieth year shall be a jubilee for you; do not sow and do not reap what grows of itself or harvest the untended vines. For it is a jubilee and is to be holy for you; eat only what is taken directly from the fields.
"'In this Year of Jubilee everyone is to return to their own property.'"

—Leviticus 25:8–13 (NIV)

As I start to discuss the Year of Jubilee, let me lay some groundwork that you should have already noticed. The Year of Jubilee happened every 50 years and it happened right after a Sabbath year, the forty-ninth year. I think you can already see a huge problem emerging, don't you? During the Sabbath year the Israelites were not allowed to plant their crops. During the Year of Jubilee, which followed that Sabbath year, the same requirement to not plant crops was in place.

So, in essence, Israel did not have a harvest for two years in a row, then had to wait during the third year—the fifty-first year—for those crops to mature and be harvested before they could replenish their food supply. This could be a serious problem for anyone who enjoys eating a good meal or makes a living selling grain.

When Moses relayed the instructions concerning the Year of Jubilee, you can imagine the confusion it must have caused. Of course, the thought of having three years off was a nice idea, but someone had to pay for it. The first thing they asked Moses when they heard about it was, "How is that possible?"

> *You may ask, "What will we eat in the seventh year if we do not plant or harvest our crops?" I will send you such a blessing in the sixth year that the land will yield enough for three years. While you plant during the eighth year, you will eat from the old crop and will continue to eat from it until the harvest of the ninth year comes in.*
>
> —Leviticus 25:20–22 (NIV)

God answers them with an amazing answer that we are going to spend a lot of time exploring in the remaining portions of this book. He said that He was going to send such a blessing in the sixth year that it would yield enough to last the three years until the new harvest would come in after the Year of Jubilee.

God is now showing Israel a picture of more than enough which stands in stark contrast to the earth curse system of painful toil, sweat, and poverty. He wanted them to see Him as their provider and that He provides with a mighty provision.

Again, although this was a picture to them of God's provision in their own day, it was still only a picture of what Jesus would actually restore to us when He came. In the natural, there was just no way to survive those three years without someone sowing a crop. Likewise, in the natural, living under the earth curse system, there would be no way to win financially without spending your days and nights sweating it out. You just can't run fast enough to get it done.

Try taking three years off from your current job while you have outstanding obligations, and you would be mixing a sure recipe for bankruptcy. But God is trying to show them a picture of a new way, one where He provides for His people, just as Adam was provided for by all God had prepared for him during creation.

Besides what the Sabbath day and the Sabbath year showed us in regard to being free from the earth curse system and being free from debt, there are two more things that the Jubilee shows us that we need to see. Again, we see the land resting, so no sowing and reaping during this fiftieth year. Also, the people are entering the Year of Jubilee with no debt due to the preceding year being a Sabbath year. But now all land was to be returned to its original owner.

When Israel crossed over the river Jordan, each tribe and each family was given land by which they would own and produce the food and revenue they needed to survive. In essence, land was their wealth. On it they grew crops and raised their livestock. So, to have all the land given back to its original owner was giving back the ability to prosper. With no debt, it was like getting a brand-new start in life! The picture was saying that they could prosper, and it points to what Jesus did for us in the same way.

There is a third thing the Jubilee shows us and that is that all slaves were to be set free and returned to their families. This is big—no, huge. Again, the shadow says that you are no longer a slave; the reality in Christ says that you are no longer a slave but now a son or daughter in God's house with full rights to the inheritance and the prosperity of the house.

Think about what we have just learned: Jesus gave us back what Adam lost! Jesus set us free from slavery, making us sons and daughters of God and freed us from the earth curse system of painful toil and sweat, allowing God to bless the work of our hands in a mighty way.

Although Jesus paid for all these things, we still must know how to appropriate these benefits into our actual lives here in the earth realm. This is where many, many Christians miss it. Not knowing that the Kingdom of God operates by laws, most Christians believe that God arbitrarily chooses who He wants to bless.

Of course, that is not true. We all share in the Kingdom equally. Also, so many people do not know they now have legal rights as sons and daughters of God's household, and also legal benefits as citizens of God's great Kingdom! Therefore, they do not study the laws of the Kingdom, which hold the key to actually enjoying and implementing what the Bible says is theirs. I am telling you, once you learn what these pictures are showing us, huge changes will occur in your financial lives.

A gentleman in my church heard me teach about faith and how the Kingdom of God operates. He and his children studied these laws together. As the new year approached, they decided that they would exercise their legal rights in the Kingdom and believe to pay off two rental properties that they had just acquired that year. If I remember correctly, I think the total needed to pay off both homes was around $450,000.

But here was the catch: they released their faith, believing to pay off both homes before the year was over. This was a stretch, but this gentleman worked in a field where he could find enough clients, or large client contracts, that he could fund such a possibility. The family prayed together and agreed this would come to pass.

Each week, the family would review their goal and review the Scriptures that gave them the legal ground to stand on to expect such a harvest. Of course, this gentleman knew he had to do his part. As the year progressed, sure enough, a few big contracts became a possibility but all with large corporations—multimillion-dollar deals are not brought to fruition quickly.

Toward the end of the year, one corporation indicated that they would sign for the multimillion-dollar contract my friend was offering them. But the date to close on the deal kept moving. The paperwork would be prepared, then the date would be moved, and the paperwork would have to be done again, and then the date would be moved again.

It was now late fall when my friend was told that the company he was waiting to sign had been sold and new management would be stepping in to take over. My friend was floored, he knew what this meant. The incoming management team from the new company were not aware of the pending contract which, of course, was now null and void. He would have to start the process all over again with the new owners.

As he met the new management team, they seemed favorable to looking at his company's suggestions, and after reviewing it in late December, they said they wanted to move forward with it. But again, paperwork was delayed and rewritten until it was New Year's Eve. My friend received a call that they wanted to meet and sign the paperwork before the year ended, which they did. My friend made enough commission on that one deal to pay off both houses in the year he had set his faith towards.

It was only by studying the Kingdom principles that even allowed or prompted him to imagine such a lofty goal, as he had never landed such a large account before or made as much money in any previous year that would have indicated that his goal was probable. He did tell me that they had quite the party to celebrate that victory!

One of my children had another "that really happened" story. Of course, all my children have watched the Kingdom functioning their entire lives. They have all applied the principles I am discussing and have seen God do amazing things.

When they were in their twenties, they all had their cars paid for and most of them had their houses paid for or almost paid for. My oldest son, Tim, wanted to buy a house with cash. So, he sowed his seed, believing God for a great deal on a home in his price range. He also is very handy with construction, so he was not afraid to buy a fixer-upper. He spent his time looking at homes but did not find the perfect match.

One day, he was driving around and spotted a home that was for sale that he had not seen before. It was a foreclosure and as he looked at it, he knew the home needed some work, but it seemed perfect for him. He called the real estate agent and had her check on the price of the home. He could not believe his ears: $37,000. But how could that be, he thought?

The agent researched the house and told an amazing story. The house was indeed a foreclosure, and it was listed for $110,000 about six months earlier. That was the foreclosure price, but the home had actually sold for $160,000 a few years earlier. Apparently, no one had shown any interest in the house for the last six months since it had been listed.

The bank then kept lowering the price, not knowing why no one had shown an interest.

But then as Tim and his real estate agent dug a little deeper, they saw why there was no interest in the house. It was listed in a completely different city with a different address and even the phone number to inquire was wrong. So, no one knew the house was there! The house, being on a small road in the country, on a dead-end street, saw no traffic. The price kept being lowered until the day that Tim spotted it. Amazing. I told Tim that the house was hidden just for him! He repainted it and did a couple things to the house and sold it for $160,000.

My daughter Amy leads worship at Faith Life Church. She and her husband Jason needed a bigger home as their family was growing from four to five. Prices were out of sight in the summer of 2017 here in Ohio, and houses that were listed were selling usually within a week. Their hope of finding a home that was large enough in the $250,000 to under $300,000 price range with 5 to 10 acres of land and a wish list possibility of water on the property, just could not be found. Ranches in the area on one acre were going for more than $200,000 that summer.

After looking at many homes, they stopped looking and prayed. Sowing a seed for direction, they told the Lord, "We are too busy to keep looking like this. You know where our house is, and we are asking you to show it to us."

One night, an interesting thing happened. Their daughter, who was four years old at the time, told them as they pulled into their home, "Mommy it is time to move." "What do you mean?" asked Amy. "It's time to move to the house with the big staircase that goes up to my room," said her four-year-old. "What house? Did you have a dream?" asked Amy. Her daughter said yes, she had.

Well, that night after they put the two kids to bed, Amy could not shake the conversation and told Jason that maybe they should look online. Yes, there was in fact a foreclosure that had just been listed, a two-story house with ten acres and a lake in front of it. The price, however, was $26,000 over the $300,000 price range they had sowed for.

They reasoned that they could always offer lower, so they called their real estate agent. The agent was leaving for Florida the next day but could possibly show them the home if they did it first thing in the morning around 9:00 a.m. Jason and Amy said they would meet her there.

The agent was late getting out to the home, but the house seemed perfect. Along with all the square footage in the home, the ten acres of land and the lake out front, everything seemed perfect. The bonus was that woods surrounded the entire property—it was breathtaking.

As they walked into the home, their daughter squealed as she ran up the huge spiral staircase straight to her room. To make a long story short, Jason and Amy said they would like to make an offer. As the agent checked on the home details, she discovered that all offers had to be received by noon that day, that was less than an hour away! If their 4-year-old had not told them the dream, and if they had not checked online that night, the house would have been gone.

They offered the asking price of $326,000 and got the bid. They were so excited. During the inspection, although the roof was in decent shape, the inspector said it would need to be replaced in five years or so. Jason had an idea. He decided to ask the bank for a lower price due to the roof needing to be replaced soon. Their agent told them to not even try because the house was being offered as is, and she had never seen a bank reduce the price on a foreclosure due to defects in the home.

But Jason and Amy felt in their spirit to write a letter and ask the bank for a reduction. You guessed it. The bank gave them the house for $296,000, less than the $300,000 they were believing God to spend. God brought the house just as they had asked him to. When they asked the appraiser what he thought the home was worth, he said $500,000. My friend, that is the double portion!

CHAPTER 3

MORE THAN ENOUGH!

Now I want to dig a little deeper into how the Sabbath rest actually works, and how to tap into it for your own life. I want to go back to our story of the Year of Jubilee and look at our text again. There we find God's answer to the people when they asked how they were to live with no harvest for three years. Good question!

> *You may ask, "What will we eat in the seventh year if we do not plant or harvest our crops?" I will send you <u>such a blessing in the sixth year that the land will yield enough for three years.</u> While you plant during the eighth year, you will eat from the old crop and will continue to eat from it until the harvest of the ninth year comes in.*
>
> —Leviticus 25:20–22 (NIV)

We see in this text that the Year of Jubilee as well as the Sabbath year preceding it were both possible because of the huge harvest that occurred in the sixth year, in this case the forty-eighth year. Remember year forty-nine was a Sabbath year and the fiftieth year was the Jubilee; both years did not allow them to plant or harvest their crops. Without that huge harvest in year forty-eight, the Sabbath rest as well as the Jubilee would not be possible. If we take a look at the manna that GOD sent Israel while they were in the wilderness, I think we can get a better picture of how this works.

The Manna

> *Each morning everyone gathered as much as they needed, and when the sun grew hot, it melted away. On the sixth day, they gathered twice as much—two omers for each person—and the leaders of the community came and reported this to Moses. He said to them, "This is what the Lord commanded: 'Tomorrow is to be a day of sabbath rest, a holy sabbath to the Lord. So bake what you want to bake and boil what you want to boil. Save whatever is left and keep it until morning.'"*

> *So they saved it until morning, as Moses commanded, and it did not stink or get maggots in it. "Eat it today," Moses said, "because today is a sabbath to the Lord. You will not find any of it on the ground today. Six days you are to gather it, but on the seventh day, the Sabbath, there will not be any."*

Nevertheless, some of the people went out on the seventh day to gather it, but they found none. Then the Lord said to Moses, "How long will you refuse to keep my commands and my instructions? <u>Bear in mind that the Lord has given you the Sabbath; that is why on the sixth day he gives you bread for two days.</u> Everyone is to stay where they are on the seventh day; no one is to go out." So the people rested on the seventh day.

—Exodus 16:21–30 (NIV)

This passage is telling us how the manna came down from heaven each day to feed the people, but they could not save it from day to day, as it would rot very quickly. Only on the sixth day, they could gather it and keep it overnight without it spoiling. The manna would not appear on the seventh day, the Sabbath, so God gave them that provision on the sixth day. So, I think it is obvious, the provision for the Sabbath was only possible because the people received a double portion on the sixth day.

Do you see it? This is so important that I am going to ask you to write this down.

THE SABBATH REST IS IMPOSSIBLE WITHOUT THE DOUBLE PORTION (more than enough)!

Let me put it in a different context. Unless you have more than enough, you will never have rest from the running and sweating of the earth curse system. As Drenda and I tell people everywhere we go, "Unless you fix the money thing you will never discover your destiny!" Why? Because without more than enough you will not have options, and you will be a slave to survival your entire life.

Poverty, survival, and bankruptcy are not your destiny. You are to be the lender and not the borrower, the head and not the tail! This abundance is what the Kingdom looks like; this is the Sabbath rest, more than enough. The double portion!

> *The Lord will grant you abundant prosperity—in the fruit of your womb, the young of your livestock and the crops of your ground—in the land he swore to your ancestors to give you.*
>
> *The Lord will open the heavens, the storehouse of his bounty, to send rain on your land in season and to bless all the work of your hands. You will lend to many nations but will borrow from none. The Lord will make you the head, not the tail. If you pay attention to the commands of the Lord your God that I give you this day and carefully follow them, you will always be at the top, never at the bottom.*
>
> —Deuteronomy 28:11–13 (NIV)

I know what you are thinking: "Boy, that sure would be nice, Gary, but my life looks nothing like that right now." That's all right; we are not looking backwards, but we are looking to what God says and expecting what the Kingdom says about us. Without the proper picture, knowing what our lives are supposed to be like, we will fall for the tricks and traps and the perverted thinking of the earth curse. Faith is staying in agreement with what God says, not our circumstances.

Your life can be defined as having more than enough. You may be skeptical of this, but this is where you are headed: more than enough. Not because I am showing you the latest, hottest money-making scheme, but because as a child of God, it is your legal right to enjoy the goodness and the prosperity of your Father's house.

The concept of the double portion—having more than enough—may seem impossible to envision compared to where you see yourself at this moment in your life. But that is where you need to start your journey to freedom—in your thinking. Unless your thoughts agree with the Word of God, you will never enjoy His benefits.

FAITH IS STAYING IN AGREEMENT WITH WHAT GOD SAYS, NOT OUR CIRCUMSTANCES.

So, lift your eyes from what you see around you and set them on what God says is yours in His Kingdom. Stop arguing with what God is saying because you do not see it in your life. Instead, start arguing with your circumstances, using the Word of God and believing that your circumstances must line up with all that God says is yours.

I am just a guy, just like you, that simply did what I am telling you to do. Believe what God says! God's Word cannot fail, and it will bring a change to any circumstance. For instance, here is an email I received from a listener who was skeptical. She had heard it all before, she says. Or had she?

"I am going to try to put 22 years of struggling in as few sentences as possible. Both my husband and I grew up in Christian families and attended church regularly. We were even involved in youth, Sunday school, etc. When we got married, our first year financially was good; that was over 22 years ago. Since then, the 'money thing' was a constant source of pain and struggle, and my faith was always wavering because I could not understand why what the Scriptures said was supposed to happen, didn't. If God's word was eternal and imperishable and He is the same yesterday, today and forever, then what gives? Either He was a martyr, a liar, or a lunatic!

"Fast forward to January 28, 2013. I told my husband, either God shows up or I walk away…I was done with church and God.

"When I left the house to run a few errands, my husband finally heeded to the Holy Spirit's urging and called a dear friend of ours to talk. After he finished, she said that she had something for us to listen to: Gary Keesee. She shared her testimony of what happened to her. So, when I got home my husband told me what she had said and that he was going over the next day to pick up the CD.

"I don't know what happened (because I had heard enough from pastors and teachers about all the 'spiritual stuff'), but I called her up, and asked if she was available that evening. In the midst of a very snowy night, I managed to get to her house. While I was driving, I told God, 'This had better be it!' The next day we started listening to the recording and the both of us were completely overwhelmed. It all started to make sense. All those verses: faith, holding fast to your confession. All the pieces of the puzzle were finally in place. We had heard about the Kingdom a few years back, <u>BUT</u> no one bothered to teach the PROCESS…how to get to the 'THERE IT IS'!

"You did.

"So immediately we put into practice what we learned. We needed money for our mortgage payment. It was Thursday and my husband had finished some small jobs at my parent's house. They kept asking

me how much they should give to my husband (they knew things were tough). I told them to give whatever they wanted. It wasn't enough to pay the mortgage payment, BUT... it was still only Thursday.

"On Friday, we had scheduled an appointment to meet with the friend who lent us the CDs. There was a major snowstorm, but both my husband and I wanted to sit down and talk to her about the Kingdom and how it operated.

"Before we left her home, she wanted to pray with us, and she handed us a check...the Lord had impressed on her heart to sow into our lives. That completely floored us. Then we opened the check... it was MORE THAN ENOUGH to pay the mortgage and other smaller bills!

"I told my husband this was all I needed! I took a picture of the check to remind me of God's faithfulness. Well, the enemy didn't like what he saw and immediately (and boy do I mean immediately!) tried to steal our seed. We had decided this was the truth and we were not going to speak anything that would destroy our future. He was relentless...but we kept our heels buried in and our shield up.

"Now before I go on, I need you to understand that I was a hardheaded Italian who was fed up with the

'prosperity teachings' I had heard...and my husband knew this. The true miracle was that I fully grasped it and held on to it. Sometimes my husband looks at me and wonders what the heck happened!

"We released our faith and sowed for our construction company in March 2013 to receive an immediate contract of $150,000 to pay off overdue bills, taxes, etc. On April 5, 2013, we received two contracts totaling $450,000 in ONE DAY! This was only two months since we began to apply the Kingdom principles.

"We got our children involved and they saw the 'there it is.' Now they've made their own list and sown from their piggy banks to seed for what they want. We have verses in every room and our 5-year-old goes to them and declares, 'I believe I have received it'.

"We are so grateful that we now have more money to give, and that we are one day closer to being debt free and being able to complete our assignments!

"Thank you, Pastor Gary, for taking the time to reply to emails that I had sent you. We understand that your time is limited and the fact that you took the time to do this shows how much you want to share this incredible message of God's great Kingdom."

I get emails like this every day. People like you and I are discovering the truth about who they are in Christ, learning how the Kingdom of God functions, and enjoying the benefits. So how did Drenda and I discover the principle of the double portion? Let me tell you the story.

When Drenda and I began to learn the laws and principles from the Kingdom of God, our lives were radically transformed as I told you in the first part of this book, from living hand to mouth, dealing with panic attacks, antidepressants, and extreme hopelessness, to a life of purpose and provision. We saw things happen over and over again that made us stop and say, "Did you see that?" Wow! We would constantly see the Kingdom of God operate just like the Bible said, and we would ask questions: how or why did that happen, what principle did we tap into?

Although we were enjoying more than enough, we really did not see the double portion as clearly as the stories I am going to show you. We were enjoying the double portion; we just did not know to actually call what we were seeing the double portion until God kept increasing our understanding of it. Before I explain how God helped us understand the double portion in a greater way, I want to review our key Scripture again.

> **There remains, then, a Sabbath-rest for the people of God; for anyone who enters God's rest (faith) also rests from their works, (the earth**

curse system of painful toil and sweat; survival)
just as God did from his (because He was
finished).

—Hebrews 4:9–10 (NIV)

(The words in parentheses are taken from my notes; they are not part of the Scripture.)

By now you know that this Sabbath rest is a promise to every New Testament believer in Christ and it is not just an Old Testament thing. You also now know that the Sabbath is not possible without having more than enough, or as we saw in Exodus chapter 16, the double portion.

Please do not confuse walking in the double portion to mean that you will in every case have a huge cash surplus on hand when God asks you to move on a project. There have been times in my life when Jesus told me to move forward on a project when I did not have any of the money in the bank. I realized later that God was never nervous about the money and knew where it would come from. But He did not allow it to manifest, lest the enemy try to steal it before it was actually needed.

Let me caution you, only make a decision to move forward in a situation like that if you are sure you have heard from the Holy Spirit to do so. Again, unless Jesus tells you to move forward on a project without the funds in place, do not move forward on it, wait until the timing of God and the provision to be available.

In general, we as believers are called to live out of the financial overflow of our lives. We are not paupers, but able to be generous on every occasion just as our Father is. I only mention this because I have received so many emails from people telling me they jumped out there and missed God's timing. Listen, just because God shows you something does not mean it is time to move on it. Many times, He shows you something to give you direction and time for preparation. In my experience, timing is just as important as hearing direction.

NOTE: The stories I am about to tell you are true. As you will see, God was very serious about helping Drenda and I understand the Sabbath of Hebrews chapter 4 and the double portion. He is very passionate about it—VERY! I want you to understand that I am not someone who is materialistic and am very content with what I have. But in the following stories, you will see just how intent God was in helping me understand the double portion and His Kingdom. I at first told Him that I felt uneasy telling the following stories, but He said, "You will tell them because they are not about you but about Me!" And I have been telling them ever since.

When Jesus began His ministry in His hometown after He had been baptized in the river Jordan by John the Baptist, and after the forty days and nights in the wilderness, He went into His local synagogue and picked up the scroll of Isaiah and turned to the sixty-first chapter and read.

*He went to Nazareth, where he had been brought
up, and on the Sabbath day he went into the
synagogue, as was his custom. He stood up to read,
and the scroll of the prophet Isaiah was handed
to him. Unrolling it, he found the place where it is
written:*

"The Spirit of the Lord is on me,
  because he has anointed me
  to proclaim good news to the poor.
*He has sent me to proclaim freedom for the
prisoners*
  and recovery of sight for the blind,
to set the oppressed free,
  to proclaim the year of the Lord's favor."
*Then he rolled up the scroll, gave it back to the
attendant and sat down. The eyes of everyone in
the synagogue were fastened on him. He began by
saying to them,* **"Today this scripture is fulfilled in
your hearing."**

—Luke 4:16–21 (NIV)

This is an amazing moment in time. The year of the Lord's
favor is the Year of Jubilee, and Jesus is saying that this
prophetic word, regarding the Jubilee has come and He is
it. What the shadow of the Sabbath, the Sabbath year, and
the Jubilee were showing us in a picture was now here as a
reality! All three of those pictures depended on the double
portion to be a reality. Now that reality, the double portion
has come, and it is yours!

Jesus is your Sabbath rest, and He is your double portion! If you have read any of my previous books, you know that the Lord taught me a lot about the Kingdom through deer hunting. In fact, deer hunting was the vehicle that God used to first catch my attention with the Kingdom. So, it was no surprise that God would use deer hunting again to show me the double portion.

If you have not read any of my deer hunting stories, let me just give you a review. I had been deer hunting for a number of years with no success. Although I was putting time and money into my efforts, I ended up with no success and no venison. To be quite honest, I never even had a shot.

This particular year, as I was thinking about the upcoming deer hunting season, God spoke to me and said, "Why don't you let Me help you with your deer hunting this year!" Of course, I had no idea what that meant, but He told me to take a check, and write, "for my 1987 buck" on it in the memo section along with a certain amount of money and then mail it to a ministry He was directing me to send it to. He also told me to have Drenda and I lay our hands on that check and claim Mark 11:24 as we prayed over it. This was the first time we had ever done that.

Mark 11:24 says, *"Therefore I tell you, whatever you ask for in prayer, believe that you have received it, and it will be yours."*

To make a long story short, I went out to a totally unfamiliar piece of property that year and had my buck in about 40 minutes. Drenda and I have followed these steps for the last thirty-eight years, and I have always harvested my deer in 30 to 60 minutes every year since then. Through the years I have seen God do some pretty amazing things while hunting, and I had learned quite a few lessons about the laws of the Kingdom through hunting as well.

(All of those early stories are recorded in my book *Faith Hunt* which you can get at Amazon.)

I usually prefer to bow hunt in the warm fall colors than to hunt in the cold gun season here in Ohio. The limit on the number of deer you can harvest is quite generous in Ohio at six deer in any given year. I have never had to harvest that many deer to feed my family. My freezer is usually pretty full with two or three deer a year.

To appreciate what I am about to tell you, you need to know that while hunting all those years, I had never shot two deer from the same tree in the same morning or evening hunt. By the way, if you are not a hunter, yes, we bow hunt from a tree stand. Typically, when I killed a deer, I would leave the woods and come back out another day and take another one. But the Lord wanted to teach me something on this particular evening hunt.

It was one of those perfect fall hunting days, a bit of cloud cover and a light drizzle dampened the ground from time to time. It was a Sunday evening and I was a bit tired from conducting multiple church services that morning and I was looking forward to being in the woods.

Drenda was heading out to do some shopping for a few things and she and I had agreed that this would be a good night to put some venison in the freezer. I was putting my camo on and gathering up my things as she went out to the car. I came outside just as she was starting the car to pull out. As she started the car, she rolled the window down and said to me, "double portion."

I do not know why she said that, although later she said that she heard the Lord say that to her at that moment and felt led to tell me that. We had sown for three deer that year, and this was the first day out hunting for that season. I gave her a quick kiss and told her I agreed, and I headed out toward our woods.

I hunt on my own property, so I was very familiar with where I was headed. As I climbed up into my tree stand, I gave my grunt call a couple of blows, and within 15 minutes, a large 8-point buck came running in. I took a forty-yard shot and my buck was down. That was awesome!

I climbed down and walked out to the buck but then I remembered what Drenda had said about the double portion, so I left the buck where he had fallen and walked back to my tree and climbed back up into the stand. I thought with all the commotion that I had made getting down, walking around, and then walking back to the stand and climbing up, not to mention all the scent I had probably scattered around, in the natural there would be a slim chance of another kill in the few remaining minutes of legal shooting light. But within 15 minutes of being in the tree, a button buck walked directly under my tree and I dropped him with a perfect shot.

Wow, two shots and two deer in a row from the same tree. I had never done that before. That caught my attention, and I knew it was the double portion Drenda had spoken of.

For the next three years I had the same experience: every time I went out bow hunting, I would now get two deer from the same tree minutes apart. I knew this was not normal, and I began to dwell on the double portion, realizing that once again God was teaching me yet another lesson about the Kingdom of God.

I have always loved guns and, of course, I love to hunt. I have my own collection of guns that I use for hunting, and I was pretty happy with the guns I owned. Drenda and I have 60 acres of land with about 25 acres of woods and another 15 acres of marsh. During any given fall, the marsh can be dry or full of water depending on how wet the summer was.

This particular year we had quite a wet summer, so the marsh was full of water as the fall duck season came in. There were always ducks coming into the marsh any year there was water, but I had not paid much attention to them. But this year there were large flocks coming into the marsh because the water was so high. I could not resist. Although I never set out to hunt them in the past, I thought I would go down to the marsh and try some duck hunting.

Well, the hunting was great. There were ducks everywhere, and I had a few duck dinners that year. While hunting ducks that year, I found that many times the ducks were passing just out of shotgun range. I was using my everyday all-around shotgun that I usually used for rabbits and pheasants, but as the ducks flew just outside of shotgun range, I remembered that I had heard of a newer type of shotgun that was designed just for duck hunting. They were camouflaged and were able to shoot the new duck loads that carried a much larger load of shot, enabling much longer shots.

I remember thinking I should check into them sometime. Well, it just happened that I was in a local sporting goods store a month after the duck season ended when I spotted a rack of guns labeled "waterfowl guns." I looked at them for a while, but with a $2,000 price tag and the fact that I would not need the gun for another 10 months when duck season reopened, I decided to wait on the purchase. Without thinking, I said out loud, "Lord, I'll take that one."

I did not think much about it as I left the store, but a few weeks later I was speaking at a corporate sales meeting— not a church meeting—a corporate sales meeting. At the end of my presentation, the CEO thanked me for speaking and said, "We wanted to thank you for speaking tonight with a gift." I was in shock as he brought out the exact shotgun I had looked at in the sporting goods store only a few weeks earlier.

My words, "Lord, I'll take that one," and the fact that I had given guns away in the past, brought that harvest. That gun showing up was amazing for sure, but it is not the main story I want to focus on. But it did prompt the story I want to tell you.

After that gun showed up, and I realized how I had put that harvest into motion, I thought for a moment one day about any other guns I would like to own. After all, I had sown dozens of guns, so I thought I would experiment with the laws of the Kingdom.

The only gun that I did not have in my collection was an over/ under shotgun. They are beautiful shotguns, and usually they are not cheap. So, I said, "Lord I would like to have one of those nice over/under shotguns!"

About a month later I received a call from a partner of the ministry, and he said that he wanted to buy me a shotgun and asked me what kind of shotgun I wanted. I told him of my desire for an over/under and he said he would send one by mail. Well, a few days later I received two beautiful over/under shotguns in the mail. Just gorgeous!

Notice that I received two shotguns. Wow, I thought. I called the partner up and thanked him for the beautiful shotguns he had sent. In a few days he sent two more. When I called to thank him again, he said, "I was so impressed that you actually called me personally to thank me, I wanted to send you two more." I was overwhelmed with the gifts, but I was beginning to see a pattern here: two shotguns each time? Sounds like the double portion.

About a month later, I was teaching at a church in the morning, and I was to teach in the same city at a different church that night. After the morning service, a man walked up to me and said, "I am going to send you a beautiful Browning semi-automatic shotgun I have." And he did. Again, I was thrilled.

Strangely, in the evening service at the other church, a man walked up to me and said, "I brought a brand-new rifle that is still in the box that I want to give you." It was a beautiful scoped out Marlin 30-30, a gun that I have often admired but have never owned. Again, I was surprised but I was catching on: the double portion.

Not a few weeks after that, the same thing happened; two more shotguns showed up at my office. Well, all I can say is, I am a man blessed with great shotguns for sure. But like every story I tell, I always ask, how did that happen? Of course, I have already told you that I have sown many guns in the past but never said, "I'll take that one, Lord," until now. This is the sickle principle you will find in the book of Mark.

> He also said, "This is what the kingdom of God is like. A man scatters seed on the ground. Night and day, whether he sleeps or gets up, the seed sprouts and grows, though he does not know how. All by itself the soil produces grain—first the stalk, then the head, then the full kernel in the head. **_As soon as the grain is ripe, he puts the sickle to it, because the harvest has come._**"
>
> —Mark 4:26–29 (NIV)

Without taking the time to really dig into that principle, basically it is telling us how faith is produced in our spirit, and when we are in agreement with heaven, faith is there. Once faith is there, we can release that agreement here in the earth realm and harvest our faith. I call it the sickle principle.

But beyond the sickle principle, I was tapping into the double portion in a very distinct and obvious way, and I knew the Lord wanted to teach me something about the double portion that He was making very clear. I believe so many of us have missed this very important aspect of reaping from the Kingdom, and I wanted to learn all I could about how this worked.

A few weeks after I received those two guns I just mentioned, I was teaching at one of my conferences, and as I was going on stage to teach this session, my cell phone went off. It was my secretary, stating that there were two boxes there for me. When I got home—you guessed it—there were two guns for me, and this time, there was a lightweight 20-gauge shotgun for Drenda and some cash for her to spend.

Now these stories happened about six years ago, and no guns have shown up since that time. But this year, I began teaching about the Sabbath rest again in January, and in January, the men's group of my church surprised me and gave me two guns.

Then in February, a lady asked me if I wanted to support their cause and I said, "Sure." She told me that her organization would be holding a raffle for two guns for those that supported them. Well, I won both drawings and was given a new 350 Legend and a Henry .22 lever-action rifle, two guns that I did not own but had wanted.

So, yes, I am overflowing with guns! How? Not by my own strength or my money, but by the grace of God, the double portion! But it was just amazing to me that God brought two more gun stories this year when I began to review the Sabbath rest. I believe it is because God is so passionate about the church understanding what He wants to do for us, and to encourage me to continue preaching and teaching the Sabbath rest.

Back in 2019 and 2020, when we were remodeling a new campus that we had purchased, we needed a couple million dollars for the project which we did not have at the time. During that entire project, two one-ounce silver dollars would show up in the weekend offering. They showed up every week throughout the entire construction project, and the money to complete the project came in as well. God was reminding me that He was taking care of the project's need for money and He did.

When we completed the project, the silver coins stopped. But this January, as I was teaching about the Sabbath, again I mentioned these silver coins. When I drove home from that service, there was a small box at my gate from Federal Express. I did not even know they delivered on Sunday. When I opened the box, there was no name but there were two one-ounce silver coins. I checked the date they were shipped, and it was the previous Thursday, days before I mentioned them.

I had not mentioned the silver coins for probably three years or more, yet as I am stepping into teaching the Sabbath rest again, they showed up. I feel that God is once again making it very clear that He wants this taught. By the way, I received another package with two silver coins in it the same week. Again, it had been shipped before I started that new series at church!

Going back to the year when I had received all those shotguns, God continued to surprise me. The following story continued to confirm that God really wanted me to get this. This story has to do with the desire that Drenda and I had to own a Cadillac Escalade. At that time, we owned a Honda Pilot and were content with it. But the church rented an Escalade for a women's conference, and Drenda and I drove it around for a bit. We loved it and said to each other that we should get one, and we decided that we wanted the shorter version and the pearl white color.

We did not tell anyone about our desire, but a week or so later, my phone rang, and the man on the phone, who goes to my church, said, "Gary, I want to buy you and Drenda a Cadillac Escalade. What color would you like?" Well, I was taken aback for a minute, but said we really like the pearl white version the best. After I thanked him, he said that he would let me know when he had it.

About a month later he called and said he had the Escalade. Drenda and I met him, and sure enough, there sat a pearl white, short-version Escalade. It was gorgeous! The gentleman from the church then walked up and said, "I am sorry, I tried to find the long version, but I could not find one." We told him that is exactly what we told the Lord we wanted: the short version. And again, in this story, I need to mention that Drenda and I have given several cars away before and had not really put a clear demand on our faith as to what we were believing to reap from that giving. That is an amazing story! But it is what happened next that really caught my attention.

We had been driving this Escalade for about a year and a half when the shotguns started showing up. One day, I noticed that the "check engine" light came on. No big deal, I thought, but I wanted to have it checked out, so I had a dealer take a look at it. They said it was really not an issue. The sensor was picking up a tiny bit of oil in the exhaust, but it would not cause a problem. The engine would last as long as I wanted to drive it.

I asked them, "Why would it be picking up some oil?" My Escalade had a custom after-market exhaust system installed, and they thought that could be a reason why the sensor was reacting. Again, they said the engine itself was fine, and I should expect it to last a long time.

In a casual conversation with the man who had given me the vehicle one day, I mentioned the sensor light issue. He said, "Yes, I have seen that happen with some other GMC vehicles. In fact, it is quite common in the older ones." He went on to say that it would not affect the car in any way and that I should be able to drive the vehicle for the next 10 years or longer with no problem.

He knew that Drenda and I have a house in Florida that I had just purchased, and I was stunned as he then said, "I will tell you what. You drive this one down to Florida and use it down there, and I will buy you another one to drive up here in Ohio." Yes, I now have two pearl white, short-version Escalades that are perfect in every way, other than the sensor light that comes on once in a while in the first one. They are both perfect in every way! Again, it was one of those "Did you see that?" moments. Drenda and I have to pinch ourselves as we drive those beautiful vehicles. We did not pay for either one of those vehicles. But in this case, we knew it was the double portion.

I am not telling you these stories to brag in any way, but friend, I am blessed! I am enjoying the double portion, which is, as you now know, having more than enough. I have a gun safe full of guns, which are more than enough. I have two identical Escalades that I did not pay for. I think you would agree that is more than enough! And it is not that I am encouraging you to seek material things; I am not. I hold things loosely, and I do not worship stuff or pursue it. I pursue the King and His Kingdom, but in the Kingdom, I find more than enough, the double portion!

Wait, I am not done testifying of the Lord's goodness and the double portion just yet.

That same year we took a trip to Quebec City in Canada in December, right before Christmas. It was so awesome there. The thing I was impressed with was all the fur. It seemed that every store had fur coats, fur hats, fur gloves, and boots for sale. Canada is known for fur, and I loved it. When I was younger, I made part-time money trapping muskrats and mink. In one store, I admired the furs and told Drenda, you know I would not mind having a fur coat of my own; I just love fur. That was all that was said.

When we arrived back in Columbus and walked into our house, there on our kitchen counter were two boxes. As we opened them, we found they contained beautiful black mink coats, one for a man and the other for a woman. They were gorgeous. The receipt left in the boxes amounted to $10,000. Again, we were shocked.

Later, at Drenda's birthday party, she received two Louis Vuitton purses. Not from me, but from two different individuals. As you know, these are high-end purses, and they are not cheap. God was making sure we got the message. We had not paid for, or asked anyone about, any of those items that showed up!

In reference to the Florida house I mentioned. My wife has wanted a beach home for the last twenty years. No, let me rephrase that: she has wanted one forever! She just loves the ocean! Anyway, she has been watching ocean property for years.

In the past, when there was a great deal on a home she liked, our money would be tied up in ministry projects, and we would wait. Well, this year I was praying in the basement as I was riding my stationary bike. Suddenly, the Lord impressed on me in a very strong way to tell Drenda to go to Florida, to that town she has desired to have a home in, and tell her to buy her ocean home this week. Wow, this week?

There was a strong urgency in my spirit when I heard that. So, I told Drenda what the Lord had said to me, and we contacted a friend of ours who lived in that city to see if she would want to drive Drenda around for a few days to look at houses. She said she would love to. So Drenda went online and made a list of about 25 homes she wanted to look at.

Once there, Drenda narrowed her list of 25 house down to five that were a possibility, and one that she said she loved. At this point, I flew down and joined her and she showed me the five houses and the one she loved. We narrowed the five to two, the one she loved and another house that was very nice, but not as nice as the one she loved.

I will have to admit when I saw the house that she loved, I knew it was Drenda, and we ended up putting an offer on it. The owner accepted our offer and we were now in contract to close on our new home.

A few weeks after we were in contract to buy the house, and as we were home in Ohio just resting, Drenda gasped and said, "That's my house!" "I know," I said. "This is your house. God told me that I was to buy you your ocean home the week I sent you to the ocean." "No," she said. "You do not understand, that is my house."

She went on to explain that she had been looking for homes for a number of years in that area and one day she saw a picture of the house we were buying in a real estate ad. When she saw it, she loved it. She loved everything about it: the Spanish Mediterranean architecture, the floor plan, the location, everything. She remembers putting her finger on that picture and saying, "Lord, I want that house!"

But she knew that house was too expensive, and we had already committed our cash to other projects, so she kept looking at houses that were in our price range at the time. But no other house clicked, and we never got to the point of actually putting a contract on one. We just did not have peace yet about a house.

You should also know that we had sown seed for an ocean beach house in this town over two years earlier. Our confession during this time was that we have a beach house in this town, we already have it. We received it the day that we sowed for it. I can remember the exact spot and moment that we held hands and came into agreement on behalf of Drenda's ocean beach house.

But now, as we were in contract, Drenda suddenly remembered the picture she had seen two years ago and realized that this was the same house, her house! After investigating the history of the house, we found out that the owner had indeed tried to sell the house a few years earlier, but it did not sell, and he took it off the market. That was when Drenda had seen the picture of the house in a real estate listing.

But the owner had decided to list it again and this explains why I had a sudden urgency to send Drenda to the ocean with the instructions, "You are to buy a house this week." She will tell you that is not how I usually spend money. Timing is everything. This time, my money was not involved with other projects and was available for the house. I am sure that there were many people looking at that house, and that was the reason for the urgency. Amazingly, the price had not gone up from the price listed two years earlier when she first saw it. I believe God was holding it for her!

But here is the double portion part of the story. While our house was in contract waiting to close, we received a call from Drenda's mother. They have owned a home in Canada for the last 32 years. We have been there a number of times over the years and loved the home and the location. The home is on an island right on the water. In fact, the ocean is about thirty feet from the back deck.

Drenda's parents were getting older and decided that they did not want the upkeep and expense of a home so far away. They came to us and asked us if we had any interest in buying it and I said, no. It was a thirty-one-hour drive from Ohio, and although I loved the place, I just did not see it being somewhere I could get to that often due to the travel time.

So, they listed the house with a real estate agent, but after having it on the market for two years, no buyer showed serious interest. So now, while we were waiting to close on our ocean beach house, they called and explained that they had tried to sell the home without success, and would be willing to cut the price in half if we wanted to buy it and keep it in the family.

As I thought about it, my children had grown up going there, and it is a beautiful place. So Drenda and I prayed about it and said we would take it. We had just enough cash on hand to make the purchase. Besides that, we had purchased a plane for my company the previous year, which allowed us to get there in five hours instead of the thirty-one hours it required by car. That made going there a lot more feasible.

After we closed on both houses, I was sitting in my office one day when suddenly it hit me: wait a minute, this is the double portion! My wife had been dreaming of an ocean home for years. But now, in the space of two months, she gets a home that is in the southern part of the United States, which is warm in the winter but too hot to really use in the summer. But the home in Canada is the perfect temperature in the summer, but too cold in the winter. We realized that she now has an ocean house for both seasons. Incredible. We definitely said, "Did you see that?" when those two closings took place. I think you would agree this looks and smells like the double portion! Amazing!

I have used several examples of how God brought two of something to Drenda and I, which I know God used to let us clearly see the double portion in operation. But I want to make sure that you do not think the double portion is limited to having two of something. In actuality, the double portion is simply having more than enough. God was using these very distinct examples of two of something to catch my attention to the double portion. So, no matter what it is, having it abundantly supplied is the double portion.

I hope you are catching the reality of the double portion and the Sabbath rest. Life is so amazing in the Kingdom! As I write this chapter, I am sitting in our home in Canada, looking out the window at the ocean. There are seagulls and ducks playing along the shore only 25 yards from the house. There is peace, no striving; it is paid for and a blessing. I am on assignment, sharing the good news of my Father's Kingdom, a son in His house, a citizen of His great Kingdom, and I am enjoying the double portion!

Drenda and I could write so many stories of how the Kingdom of God and the laws that govern it have impacted our lives as well as the thousands of people that email us with their stories as well. As I said, you can read all these things in the Bible, but it is so exciting to see the Bible play out before your eyes. What we have seen and what we are enjoying is the result of our Father and His Kingdom in our lives. We share these stories because we just want you to get it! Hey, we came from nothing, and the only reason I am writing this book is for you! I want you to know how it works so that you can understand and receive all God has for you as well.

I hate poverty with a passion. Those nine years of living in constant stress and fear were a living hell on earth, literally! I hope you will remember that the Sabbath rest is yours as well as mine!

One day I told the Lord, "Lord, I do not need 15 shotguns or two Escalades and all that you have given me." He responded, "No, you do not need anything, but I wanted to stretch your poverty mindset. My Kingdom is a kingdom of abundance, and I want my people to have that. I wanted to be very sure you understood the double portion is yours."

It is amazing that everything that the Lord gave me that year was top quality, top-of-the-line. And again, it is not about having things, but He used these things, things that were top-of-the-line, to illustrate His Kingdom. To give me and you an example which says that God has all we need and desire in His Kingdom. His desire is for us to be the head and not the tail, the lender and not the borrower.

I told you that the Lord spoke to me about 2025 and beyond and said that 2025 was going to be a year of great harvest and plunder. Well, we have just covered how great harvests happen. The double portion and even a triple portion in the Jubilee Year. Those are huge harvests. As we walk in the double portion, we will walk in supernatural abundance. I did not cover in this book how to step into the double portion as it is explained in detail in my book *Your Financial Revolution: The Power of Rest*.

We are not finished yet. Great Harvests **and** Plunder are ahead!

CHAPTER 4

PLUNDER

In the last three chapters we reviewed the Sabbath rest, the Sabbath year and the Jubilee. We found out that all of them were simply shadows, or a picture, of what Jesus would bring to us in the New Covenant.

> *Therefore do not let anyone judge you by what you eat or drink, or with regard to a religious festival, a New Moon celebration or a Sabbath day. These are a shadow of the things that were to come; **the reality, however, is found in Christ.***
>
> —Colossians 2:16–17 (NIV)

I mentioned in the foreword that God spoke to me in December 2024 and told me that the body of Christ was about to enter a season of great harvest and plunder. As the word "plunder" was a word that I had never used, I was a little surprised that God would use that word concerning the future. But I looked it up and gave you the definition in the foreword: "something taken by force, theft, or fraud, often referring to the spoils of war or conquest."[1] The meaning of the word at the time was unclear to me, as I did not understand how to apply that definition to the Bible. What did that mean? It is a common word used over 140 times in the Bible, but strangely, I never really thought about it.

I spent the month of December praying and studying what God was trying to tell me. I already knew what God meant when He said 2025 and beyond would be a season of great harvest; the church would begin walking more powerfully in the revelation of the double portion. I gave you a review of that principle in the previous three chapters. But I was not sure exactly what He meant by "plunder." The definition was interesting, but I needed to see what that meant and how to walk that out. To begin, I want to go back to Luke, chapter 4 where we see Jesus in his hometown synagogue.

> *Jesus returned to Galilee in the power of the Spirit, and news about him spread through the whole countryside. He was teaching in their synagogues, and everyone praised him.*
>
> *He went to Nazareth, where he had been brought up, and on the Sabbath day he went into the synagogue, as was his custom. He stood up to read, and the scroll of the prophet Isaiah was handed to him. Unrolling it, he found the place where it is written:*

---

[1] "Plunder," *Merriam-Webster* dictionary, https://www.merriam-webster.com/dictionary/plunder.

"The Spirit of the Lord is on me,
  because he has anointed me
  to proclaim good news to the poor.
He has sent me to proclaim freedom for the
prisoners
  and recovery of sight for the blind,
*to set the oppressed free, to **proclaim the year of***
***the Lord's favor**."*

Then he rolled up the scroll, gave it back to the
attendant and sat down. The eyes of everyone in
the synagogue were fastened on him. He began by
*saying to them, **"Today this scripture is fulfilled in***
your hearing."

—Luke 4:14–21 (NIV)

As we have already studied, the year of the Lord's favor is the Year of Jubilee, and Jesus said it was fulfilled at that moment! Boy, would I have loved to be there that day. Can you imagine what went through that room when He said that? By saying that this prophetic word in Isaiah was fulfilled that day, He was saying that He was the coming Messiah.

And since we understand that the Jubilee was a shadow or a picture of what was to come and the reality is in Christ, we know that He was saying the real Jubilee, not just the picture, was here. Everything that the picture showed us was no longer just a picture but was actually here; Jesus is our Jubilee! There is probably no other Scripture in the

Bible that carries that much punch—and as much change—as that one.

The Jubilee was showing us that through Jesus, man can live above the earth curse system of painful toil and sweat, and debt would not be needed to live. All land was given back to the original owner, meaning they got back their means to prosper, and finally, all slaves were set free.

What a party that would have been, or should we say, should have been. It seems that those who heard Him say that were not happy about what He said. The problem? He grew up in that town. He faithfully came to worship at that synagogue His entire life. Everyone knew Him there. How dare He say that He was the Messiah? In their anger, they dragged Him outside and tried to kill Him, which they were unable to do, of course.

Jesus was reading out of Isaiah 61:1–2, but there is something very interesting about how He read it. As I said earlier, He read down to verse 2, then stopped in the middle of a sentence! That's right, He stopped reading in the middle of a sentence.

Now we know He stopped on the phrase, *"to proclaim the year of the Lord's favor,"* because He was making a point. I am He. It, meaning the Jubilee, is here!

But what about the rest of the sentence? What about the rest of the chapter? It is here, in the remainder of that one sentence that we find something that you may have never seen before. Something that, if truly understood, would change how we deal with Satan and his demons, not settling for defeat and loss, but instead demanding spiritual justice. Let's go to the place where Jesus was reading and see what the rest of that sentence said.

> *The Spirit of the Sovereign Lord is on me,*
> *because the Lord has anointed me*
> *to proclaim good news to the poor.*
> *He has sent me to bind up the brokenhearted,*
> *to proclaim freedom for the captives*
> *and release from darkness for the prisoners,*
> *to proclaim the year of the Lord's favor*
> **_and the day of vengeance of our God._**
> —Isaiah 61:1–2a (NIV)

Stop everything. If Jesus said that the first part of this sentence was fulfilled in His coming, then I can assume that the second part of that sentence is here as well. Let's begin by a simple definition of the word "vengeance."

Vengeance: punishment inflicted, or retribution exacted for an injury or wrong.[2]

Let's dive a bit deeper with that explanation and look at the word "retribution."

---

[2] "Vengeance," *Merriam-Webster* dictionary, https://www.merriam-webster.com/dictionary/vengeance.

Retribution: redress, remedy or to set right an undesirable or unfair situation.[3]

In a legal sense, the simplest definition of that word "vengeance" is to set right an undesirable or unfair situation. If someone ran over your fence, your insurance company would bring remedy or retribution, making things right. So, if we read Isaiah verse 2 again with that definition, it could read like this: *"to proclaim the year of the Lord's favor **and to bring retribution and remedy to those that have suffered loss at the hands of the enemy."***

Let's go to the Word of God for an example of this principle. I want to go to a chapter that we read at Christmas every year. For the most part, most of the Christmas stories we read do not include this part of Isaiah chapter 9, but they should.

> *The people walking in darkness*
> *have seen a great light;*
> *on those living in the land of deep darkness*
> *a light has dawned.*
> *You have enlarged the nation*
> *and increased their joy;*
> *they rejoice before you*
> *as people rejoice at the harvest,*
> *as warriors rejoice*
> *when dividing the plunder.*

[3] "Retribution," Collins English Dictionary, https://www.collinsdictionary.com/us/dictionary/english/retribution

For as in the day of Midian's defeat,
*   you have shattered*
the yoke that burdens them,
*   the bar across their shoulders,*
*   the rod of their oppressor.*
Every warrior's boot used in battle
*   and every garment rolled in blood*
will be destined for burning,
*   will be fuel for the fire.*
For to us a child is born,
*   to us a son is given,*
*   and the government will be on his shoulders.*
And he will be called
*   Wonderful Counselor, Mighty God,*
*   Everlasting Father, Prince of Peace.*
Of the greatness of his government and peace
*   there will be no end.*
He will reign on David's throne
*   and over his kingdom,*
establishing and upholding it
*   with justice and righteousness*
*   from that time on and forever.*
The zeal of the Lord Almighty
*   will accomplish this.*

—Isaiah 9:2–7 (NIV)

Most of the Christmas stories we read or hear in church start reading in verse 6: "*For to us a child is born, to us a son is given, and the government will be on his shoulders.*"

No doubt, verses 6 and 7 are powerful and are so full of revelation regarding who Jesus is, and the mighty government he is setting up on the earth. But what about the preceding five verses? They are also extremely powerful and rich in revelation concerning the impact that Jesus is bringing to the earth, to you, and to me. The greatest thing you see as you scan those first five verses is it appears that a great battle is over.

> *Every warrior's boot used in battle*
>   *and every garment rolled in blood*
> *will be destined for burning,*
>   *will be fuel for the fire.*
> *For to us a child is born,*
>   *to us a son is given,*
>   *and the government will be on his shoulders.*
>   —Isaiah 9:5–6a (NIV)

The Holy Spirit compares Jesus's victory over Satan to the battle Israel fought against Midian. Of course, there is no comparison between the two as far as impact is concerned. But the Holy Spirit does use this battle to help us understand some of the impact and benefits that Jesus's victory over Satan has on us as people.

Jesus's victory over Satan, as we have been saying, brings us the Sabbath rest of the Jubilee, but also vengeance. Again, we are focusing on the vengeance part of that promise.

First of all, you will notice that there is a difference in the prophetic time frames of these two benefits. First, the Bible refers to the Jubilee as "the year" of the Lord's favor. And in fact, the picture of the Jubilee lasted a year. But the day of vengeance is not referenced in the same way. It is noted as the "day" of vengeance. The difference is that the Year of Jubilee spoke in terms of a place where you are dwelling, a description of how you would be living, compared to the day of vengeance, which speaks of action—immediate action.

The book of Isaiah speaks of a battle being over, and it is referencing a battle that took place in Judges chapter 6, the battle with the Midianites. Originally, God gave Israel over to Midian for seven years because of their sin and rebellion against Him. The Midianites would come to steal Israel's harvest and their livestock.

The oppression was so great that the people of Israel abandoned the lush valleys and hid from the Midianites in the mountains. God used someone by the name of Gideon, who was unknown, to lead Israel against this hoard that had invaded Israel. God was not looking for a military commander, but instead someone who would believe Him and do what He wanted done.

This was going to be God's fight, and He was not looking for someone who would lean on their own strength. Gideon was the man. But this was no small task. The Bible says there were so many enemies in the land that they could not be counted. Yet, as Gideon depended on God, he and only three hundred soldiers led the charge against the invaders and defeated them.

> *For as in the day of Midian's defeat,*
>   *you have shattered*
> *the yoke that burdens them,*
>   *the bar across their shoulders,*
>   *the rod of their oppressor.*

—Isaiah 9:4 (NIV)

Isaiah compares Jesus's coming and bringing the government of heaven to earth as a deliverance, similar to the one that Israel experienced when they were set free from the oppression of Midian. Gideon, by God's spirit, shattered Midian's hold on Israel. Jesus did the same. He shattered the yoke of Satan which enslaved all of us.

To get a clear picture of this analogy, you should think of an ox that is plowing in a field. The yoke is strapped to the ox, and he is being driven by a driver with a rod to direct and motivate the ox to move forward. In the analogy, Satan and the earth curse system of labor to sustain survival is the driver, driving all of us to run after provision. Under this curse, which is what Adam ushered into the earth when he rebelled against God, people are being forced to run, to work, and sweat for survival. Through Jesus that yoke of slavery has been broken! We have been given the double portion, the Sabbath rest, which is more than enough.

Let's think about what Isaiah is saying:

> *You have enlarged the nation*
> *and increased their joy;*
> *they rejoice before you*
> *as people rejoice at the harvest,*
> *as warriors rejoice*
> *when dividing the plunder.*
>
> —Isaiah 9:3 (NIV)

The nation of Israel was hiding in fear in the hills and caves of the mountains. They had allowed the enemy to push them off of their inheritance. Although they owned the lush valley—their inheritance—they were not enjoying it at all. It was being occupied by a foreign army.

The first thing that was restored to Israel in this battle was their inheritance, their land. Losing their land meant they lost their harvest. If they wanted to be all that God wanted them to be, and have all that God wanted them to have, they would have to take back what the enemy had stolen!

It would be easy to just agree with what they saw, in the natural: the battle could not be won, the foreign armies were too many to count. Yet, legally, they already owned the best farmland around. It was theirs, but someone else was occupying it. No, they could not accept such an outcome. There were four things that they would have to realize if they ever wanted to see the promises of God in their lives:

1. Their sin and rebellion had taken them outside of the blessing of God, and they were now living outside of God's promises. They could see the ungodly occupying what should have been theirs.
2. They would never have the harvest and prosperity that God had promised as long as they allowed the enemy to occupy what was legally theirs.
3. They would have to reoccupy their land and kick the enemy out!
4. Then they would need to go <u>to the enemy's camp</u> and plunder it! Meaning they would need to go after the enemy, find their stash, and bring back all that the enemy had stolen.

Motivated by Gideon, they tore down the idols, repented before the Lord, took back their land, and regained the benefit of their inheritance, their ability to harvest. Then they plundered the enemy and took back EVERYTHING THE ENEMY HAD STOLEN! This is the destiny of the children of God.

LET ME SUM UP WHAT GOD TOLD ME. The body of Christ is moving into a season of great harvest and plunder. We will enjoy great harvest, as we discussed in the last chapter, as well as the enemy's plunder. The definition of plunder is something taken by force, theft, or fraud, often referring to the spoils of war or conquest.

Do you think the enemy has ever taken anything through theft, force or fraud, or conquest? Of course, he has! And now he has been defeated and those things, the things he has stolen or is holding that belong to someone else, can be taken back!

Catch this: the plunder that we will be picking up will not only be what the enemy has stolen from us individually, but from what he has stolen for generations. I will explain more about this later, but for now, let's be really clear about what this battle is saying regarding this season in time.

THERE WILL BE GREAT REJOICING AT THE HARVEST.

First, the Word is clear, when Jesus broke the power of Satan against us, and He shattered the earth curse system that stands against us, there will be great rejoicing at the harvest. I am not seeing just another year with a normal harvest. No, I see a supernatural ability to harvest coming to the body of Christ in this season. A picture of what I see coming can be found in Luke chapter 5.

> Simon answered, "Master, we've worked hard all night and haven't caught anything. But because you say so, I will let down the nets."
>
> When they had done so, they caught such a large number of fish that their nets began to break. So they signaled their partners in the other boat to

come and help them, and they came and filled both boats so full that they began to sink.

When Simon Peter saw this, he fell at Jesus' knees and said, "Go away from me, Lord; I am a sinful man!" For he and all his companions were astonished at the catch of fish they had taken, and so were James and John, the sons of Zebedee, Simon's partners.

—Luke 5:5–10a (NIV)

I am talking about astonishing harvests! Great harvests are coming!

Keith was tired of being a slave when he came across my TV broadcast, *Fixing the Money Thing* a few years ago. He and Kathy, his wife, were glued to the TV because they did not know there was a way out. They bought my books and CDs and listened and read over and over again. Finally, they began to dream again as God's Word changed their hopeless mindset.

I met Keith at one of my Provision conferences which I host every year, the last week in April. When we met, he began telling me how he lost his corporate job a few months back but had been listening to my teaching on the Kingdom and learning how the Kingdom works for months. He said his vision for his future slowly began to change and he realized that he did not want to find another corporate job, but he wanted to start his own business; he was convinced that God had a better plan.

Keith did not really know what he would do for a business, but he did like to work with wood. He had some wood sitting around and thought that he could make and sell furniture. But after trying it for a while, he said he knew that it was not his answer.

He also had some background in trucking, so he decided to start a truck hauling business. He had one truck and began to gather a few clients, hauling cars and anything else people needed hauled. He said in his first month he made just over $4,000 and was thrilled. That was really close to what he had been making in his corporate job, so he knew he was on the right track.

As he kept going with his one truck, he heard through a friend about a company that was looking for more truckers to deliver various commodities they were producing. He decided to check it out. He was excited as he researched the potential of driving for this new company. He and Kathy prayed about it and felt they should go that direction. This would require them to purchase a semi truck, which could haul a semi-trailer, so he did that and began to haul for this company.

I can remember Kathy emailing me with excitement not long after that. She said that she had just finished invoicing that new company for over thirty-one thousand for one week's work. As I read the email, I kind of just stopped with a sudden gasp as I saw that she said thirty-one thousand for that week's work.

The demand kept growing, so he bought two more trucks and hired two drivers. Now his business was getting more complicated, and he and Kathy realized that they were over their heads regarding administration and how to run a business. So, they hired a company to come in and train them on how to set up their company with the right processes and administration.

I got a second letter from Kathy stating that they had just broke another record. She had just invoiced the company for $72,000 for one week's work. Demand kept increasing, so they bought more trucks and hired more drivers. This was eight years ago. Keith now has forty trucks on the road for his company and is now bringing in over ten million dollars a year. Keith says he has to pinch himself remembering where he came from and where he is at today.

Oh, by the way, Keith paid cash for all those trucks! His company is debt free, and his life has drastically changed! Is he slowing down? No! He is still buying more trucks and adding more clients almost every month. Keith found out that dreams can still come true. Kathy said that they listened to the teaching on the Kingdom every day for two years at the beginning of this. They knew that they had so much religious training but no Kingdom training. They knew they had to completely relearn everything they thought they knew about God and the Kingdom of God.

Keith and Kathy now also travel the country, teaching others the Kingdom principles that changed their lives. But Keith and Kathy will tell you that they are not God's special favorites. They know that all of God's children have the same legal rights in the Kingdom that they do. And if you will take the time to learn how the Kingdom operates you can have the same kind of success they have had—amazing harvests!

Do you like payday? Well, when you step into the double portion of the Jubilee, you are going to see a great change in your finances, and you will experience great rejoicing and great harvests.

Again, let's remember what the Word says, *"For as in the days of Midian's defeat..."* (Isaiah 9:4, NIV) Meaning, in reference to Jesus ushering in this new government, we will be like those who rejoice at the harvest, and as warriors who are rejoicing when dividing the plunder. But what about this word "plunder"? We have talked for most of this book about harvest, but what about this?

Well, we have touched on it, that it is something that the enemy has stolen, and we are going to take it back. To understand exactly what this is saying, I think we should go back to that battle in Judges chapter 6 and take a look at it. Let's face it, there were many battles in the Old Testament that God could have referenced, but the Spirit of God used this one to illustrate the impact and effect Jesus would have on our lives.

> They [the Midianites] came up with their livestock and their tents like swarms of locusts. ***It was impossible to count them*** or their camels; they invaded the land to ravage it.
>
> —Judges 6:5 (NIV)

If you remember the story, Gideon and three hundred men defeated the Midianites. Gideon devised a plan by the Spirit of God to simply surround the camp with three groups and they were to uncover their torches and blow their trumpets and shout when Gideon gave the signal. This plan made it look like the enemy was surrounded by a large army and it caused the Midianites to panic. In the dark night, they could not see, and in their confusion, they began killing each other. The battle was a complete victory, and it says that after the battle, Gideon's men picked up the plunder, meaning they recovered all that the Midianites had stolen from them, **but also they were able to pick up what the enemy had stolen from others as well.**

To give you an idea how big the plunder was, the Bible says that some of the enemy army wore gold earrings, so Gideon asked each of his men to give him one earring from the plunder; the soldiers could keep everything else they had captured. The weight of the gold earrings Gideon was given came to seventeen hundred shekels, which in today's value at around $3,000 an ounce for gold would equal $2,054,417!

So, here is the truth I want you to see. Most Christians are content to run off the Midianites. Yay! The Midianites are gone, now we can go on with our lives. Hold on; not so fast. What about what the enemy has stolen? It is not enough to celebrate that the enemy is gone. Gone; great. But he is gone with your goods!

The Israelites had lost quite a lot by being overrun by the Midianites! All the harvest that they were never able to harvest and was stolen by the enemy, what about that? Well, most people would just be glad that they got their land back and can now get back to farming and moving forward. I agree that deliverance is worthy of a celebration, and especially how God was so involved with it. A great story for sure!

But what about God's vengeance?

Let's compare this story to a modern-day event that you are well aware of. Let's assume that someone runs off the road and smashes into your nice wooden fence. The car is stuck in your yard and your fence is severely damaged. The guy who ran into your fence calls the tow truck and it comes and eventually removes the car out of your yard.

We can all agree that getting the car out of your yard was great. But would we have a celebration because the car has been removed? No, of course not, we want our fence fixed, and the ruts in our yard as well. So, we call our insurance company, and they will go after his insurance company for the cost of the repairs. We want full restitution and remedy. Let me make this very clear.

We want things to be put back as they were before the car came into our yard!

In a nutshell, that is what plunder is speaking of, getting back what is lost or stolen. Let me give you another example, an example which is probably one of the best examples of this principle in the Word of God.

As most of you probably know, Israel spent about 430 years in Egypt before Moses led them out. Not all of those years were bad years. In fact, at first, they were glorious years. Joseph had interpreted Pharaoh's dream concerning the coming famine and was put in charge of all of Egypt, becoming second in command under Pharaoh. Joseph's family then moved to Egypt and were greatly honored there.

Of course, during the course of time, a new Pharaoh came into power who did not know Joseph and put the Hebrews into slavery. It is estimated that of the 430 years that Israel was in Egypt, 200 of those years were spent in slavery. It was at that point that God directed Moses to bring the Hebrews out. We find God talking to Moses about this deliverance in the third chapter of Exodus.

> *"So I will stretch out my hand and strike the*
> *Egyptians with all the wonders that I will perform*
> *among them. After that, he will let you go.*
> *"And I will make the Egyptians favorably disposed*
> *toward this people, so that when you leave you will*
> *not go empty-handed. Every woman is to ask her*
> *neighbor and any woman living in her house for*
> *articles of silver and gold and for clothing, which you*
> *will put on your sons and daughters. And so you will*
> *plunder the Egyptians."*
>
> —Exodus 3:20–22 (NIV)

Ok, let's stop for a minute. These people have been slaves for over 200 years. You would think that just leaving Egypt and being free from slavery would be enough. I mean, what a victory that would be in its own right. Especially when you see how God did it. The plagues that came on the Egyptians, forcing Pharaoh to let them go, and then to see God's deliverance at the Red Sea. I mean, do you need a more dramatic story? But going empty-handed is not how God operates, oh no. Egypt owed Israel for 200 years of forced labor. God said they were to plunder the Egyptians!

> *The Lord had made the Egyptians favorably*
> *disposed toward the people, and they gave*
> *them what they asked for; so they plundered the*
> *Egyptians.*

—Exodus 12:36 (NIV)

Was God being unfair to the Egyptians? Not at all. Let's look at our definition of the word "plunder" again.

Plunder: something taken by force, theft, or fraud, often referring to the spoils of war or conquest.[4]

All those years when the Hebrews were slaves by force with no pay—I think we could call their loss plunder. And to be sure, God was not leaving that plunder in Egypt; no sir, not a chance. They were bringing it out with them!

> He brought out Israel, laden with silver and gold,
> and from among their tribes no one faltered.
> —Psalms 105:37 (NIV)

The word "laden" means carrying a large load or burden, heavily or abundantly loaded.[5]

As these former slaves were leaving Egypt, although they had never owned any gold or silver in their lifetime and neither did their parents or their grandparents, they were now laden down with all the gold and silver they could carry! As the church, we have not been taught that we have a right to plunder. In fact, very few people even know what that is. Plunder in simple terms is demanding what the devil has

[4] "Plunder," Merriam-Webster dictionary

[5] "Laden," Merriam-Webster dictionary, https://www.merriam-webster.com/dictionary/laden

stolen to be returned. We have a right to demand remedy before our God.

Plunder infers that someone (or Satan) is holding something that you have a legal claim to. The body of Christ usually is satisfied to move on and escape the conflict, counting the losses as part of the equation, but God does not think that way. Nope, God wants justice; everything lost is to be returned!

Let me give you a personal story to illustrate.

When we first moved to Ohio from Tulsa, money was almost nonexistent. When we got here, I had to start my business all over again. That was tough. Needing to feed three children at the time, I had to have some money to hold me over as I started gaining clients. We survived on credit cards, the generosity of our relatives, and pawn shops. One day, I had to have some cash, and the only option was to pawn a couple guns that I owned.

One of them that I pawned that day was a Winchester model 75 .22 rifle. This rifle was special to me because, first, my dad gave it to me, and second, it was the first gun he had bought as a teenager. There was no way that I was going to leave it at the pawn shop, I thought. But when the time expired, I did not have the money to pay the interest or buy it back out of pawn and I lost it.

I was so upset about losing that gun. Over the years I thought about that gun, and every time I did, there was always a twinge of remorse. One day, I was thinking about it, and I told the Lord that I sure would like to find that gun and buy it back.

A year later, and this is just two years ago, I went into Cabela's and walked back to the firearms section. Cabela's has a little room near the firearms section where they sell used guns. I rarely look in that room, and I go to Cabela's only about three to four times a year, but this day I decided to take a glance in that room. I stopped in my tracks when I saw my dad's gun there.

Now I am not sure it was the one I pawned or not, but it was an exact replica of it, down to the finish and condition. Since I pawned the gun in the same town that the Cabela's was in, it could have been the same exact gun. I have been around guns all my life and I had never seen a gun like his in all those years.

I bought it and have it to this day. I even hunt with it from time to time. But this is an example of the lost being found, of what I thought I would never see again, now restored. Plunder does not have to come from a huge battle, where God has to force the enemy to let go of what it is holding. No, Jesus already won that war. It can simply be someone selling a gun to Cabela's and they just happen to put it on display where I can see it on one of the few days I come in. You do not have to do this on your own either; the Holy Spirit and the angels can do this, following your instruction.

In the gun situation, I asked the Lord to find that gun for me. I lost that gun, not out of a desire to lose it or sell it, but out of pressure and circumstances that were not all my doing.

Let me give you another example.

When Drenda and I began learning about the Kingdom of God, we saw so many stories in our lives that were just amazing and outstanding. I began to keep mementos that would always remind me of those events and how God came through in so many ways.

We saw God raise the dead, we saw tumors disappear, we saw fantastic financial stories, amazing answers to prayer, demons manifested and cast out, and so much more. For instance, when I went to the Philippines, there was a pastor there who was paralyzed and could not walk or work. He had to be carried to the front of the meeting I was holding with a group of 200 pastors. I laid my hands on him, and he was instantly healed. At that moment, the entire group of 200 pastors rushed forward for me to pray for them when they saw their friend completely and instantly restored.

Out of thanksgiving, they took up an offering for me. It was in their currency, and I think it was worth about $70 in US dollars. But I still have that offering; I never converted it to US dollars. But I kept it to remind me of that event. I also have the ring from my Albanian meeting where God called me to the nations. I have so many of those kinds of items that I have kept over the years to remind me how faithful God has been to me.

I usually never take that bag out of my safe, but a couple years ago, I was teaching, and I wanted to use it as an example. So, I took it to church with me and used it at the weekend services. Somehow, when we left church quickly to get to a lunch appointment, I left it on the table in my office. I was not too concerned as I knew my office would be locked. That Monday, I had to fly out to another meeting, so I did not get the bag. I called my office on Tuesday to check on it, and my staff said they had put it in my car after Sunday service, which I did not know. When I got home, the car was at the house, and I went to see if the bag was there and I could not find it.

I called the church again and no one had seen it. I knew that I had not had it since the Sunday services and the last time I saw it, it was on the table in the office. I searched that car over, looking in and under every part of that interior, at least three or four times. We checked with all the staff and everyone looked, but no one found the bag. I was so sad that I might have lost those precious memories. The bag was missing for six months. Finally, I asked the Lord to find it for me and bring it back to me.

One day I went out to the car and stopped for a second. I was shocked to see the bag hanging out of the pouch pocket behind the driver's seat by about five inches. I had checked that pocket probably almost a dozen times, but here it was hanging half out, just as plain as the sun coming up. I knew there was only one explanation, and that was an angel put it there for me. Don't act so shocked; I have had angels help me more than once when I could not find something. To this day, I do not know if someone stole it and then felt guilty about it and brought it back, or how it was lost. All I know is that God will bring back things that have been lost if you ask Him.

Remember the enemy's plunder is yours—don't let him keep it!

CHAPTER 5

NO, YOU DON'T, DEVIL; I'M TAKING IT BACK!

People do not despise a thief if he steals
to satisfy his hunger when he is starving.
Yet if he is caught, he must pay sevenfold,
thought it cost him all the wealth of his house.
—Proverbs 6:30–31 (NIV)

I love this Scripture as it clearly lays out God's view of justice. A thief must give back all he has stolen and return to the one that he stole from, seven times what was stolen.

Here is a story, originally told by Pastor Rod Parsley, that I think will encourage you to stand your ground against Satan and not let him steal from you. You have the legal right to say, "Put it back!"

Dr. Lester Sumrall years ago found himself in the middle of the Central American rain forest. As he went about his ministry in that region, he came across a witch doctor. In today's rock and roll Hollywood scene, this witch doctor would look like a normal man…but in those days, this was a pretty strange fellow!

In one hand, the witch doctor would hold a bull frog (always a symbol of satanic power). In the other hand, he had a mixture of human blood and alcohol which was placed in the frog's mouth. Then the witch doctor would dance, make satanic incantations and worship demon entities.

Fortunately, Dr. Sumrall wasn't raised in the modern-day school of humanistic, people-pleasing preachers. All Dr. Sumrall did was follow Jesus's biblical example. He placed his hands on the side of the witch doctor's head and said two words: **"Come out!"**

The witch doctor fell over with a thud. When he returned to his feet, the witch doctor was born again and speaking in a heavenly language and glorifying God.

Later that night, Dr. Sumrall returned to his room to go to bed. Since it was warm, and without air conditioning, he decided to open the windows while he slept.

As he lay down, a strange odor began to fill the room. Suddenly, all the sultry heat of the night disappeared from the room. A damp chill filled the place. It was so cold Dr. Sumrall began to shiver. A wind began to blow the curtains wildly on their rods. Then, the bed began to shake so violently that it moved all the way into the middle of the floor.

Well, Dr. Sumrall had enough of this! He raised up on his bed and said, "You demon spirit, I recognize you. I cast you out earlier today. In the name of Jesus Christ of Nazareth, you go now!"

Immediately, the evil presence left the room. The heat returned. The curtains laid down against the wall; the bed stopped shaking. The horrible odor left the room.

Now, most modern-day preachers would have written a book right there! They would have written seven books and told how the devil obeyed them…but, that wasn't Dr. Sumrall. Instead, he rose back up in his bed, looked out the window and shouted, "Hey devil! Get back in here!"

Immediately the curtains began to stick out on end as a wind rushed through the room. The coldness returned…the smell returned…the bed began to shake violently, and almost shook him out of bed.

Dr. Sumrall sat up in his bed and said, "Devil…When I came into this room my bed was against that wall. Now, in the name of Jesus, PUT IT BACK!"

The bed went shaking back across the room and settled down against the wall.

"Now," Dr. Sumrall ordered, "get out of here!"

Today is the day of restoration for you and the church. We are not to be content with just making the devil leave … but we are going to tell him to PUT IT BACK and restore EVERYTHING that he has stolen from us!

Now, it is time to invade the enemy's territory and take back everything that rightfully belongs to us.

Wow! Did you see that? I am telling you, the kingdom of darkness is wide open for plunder. The battle is over, Jesus already beat the devil; the battle is over. I am telling you, the walls are down.

> I will build My church, and the gates of Hades **will not overcome it.**
>
> —Matthew 16:18b (NIV)

Christians are afraid of the devil when the Bible is clear that he is completely defeated, and we can walk in the power of the Holy Spirit and God's authority. I have some friends who live in Australia and who were on the mission field in Africa. They were working in an area with a lot of voodoo and witchcraft. Dealing with demons was an almost constant occurrence. They told me that they had many witch doctors come to Jesus while they were there.

NO, DO NOT BE AFRAID OF THE ENEMY, HE HAS BEEN DEFEATED.

An interesting conversation they had with a born-again witch doctor was around the topic of demons avoiding Christians. The witch doctor said that in the spirit world, the Christians glow and the demons would try to avoid them. Should we be surprised? No, the Word of God tells us the same thing.

> *Submit yourselves, then, to God. Resist the devil, and he will* ***flee from you.***
> —James 4:7 (NIV)

That word "flee" literally means to run in terror. Also, please note who the demons want to run from—YOU! No, do not be afraid of the enemy; he has been defeated. In fact, we are not to avoid him, because behind his wall of deception are countless millions who are being held under his dominion.

No, we are not to avoid him but run toward him and plunder his kingdom. I said we are to plunder the kingdom of darkness—the walls are down; his kingdom lays wide open for plunder. The treasure? Yes, there is more wealth stored there then you can even imagine. Wealth that has been stolen from God's people. Wealth that was intended to do good. Wealth that is beyond imagination. But wealth is not the plunder our Father God is most interested in; it is the people that are being held there. And Jesus has given us, the church, a direct command—not a suggestion—but a command, to go after them.

> *He said to them, "Go into all the world and preach the gospel to all creation. Whoever believes and*

is baptized will be saved, but whoever does not believe will be condemned. And these signs will accompany those who believe: In my name they will drive out demons; they will speak in new tongues; they will pick up snakes with their hands; and when they drink deadly poison, it will not hurt them at all; they will place their hands on sick people, and they will get well."

After the Lord Jesus had spoken to them, he was taken up into heaven and he sat at the right hand of God. Then the disciples went out and preached everywhere, and the Lord worked with them and confirmed his word by the signs that accompanied it.
—Mark 16:15–20 (NIV)

Remember, Jesus already won the war and stripped Satan of his jurisdiction and authority. Now, we are on a mission to take his plunder, to take back what Satan has captured and what was lost. When Satan deceived Adam and Eve, Satan stole through deception God's highest creation: men and women. Men and women are the plunder that Satan holds today under his jurisdiction. But he also holds the wealth of the nations under his dominion.

*The devil led him up to a high place and showed him in an instant all the kingdoms of the world. And he said to him, "I will give you all their **authority and splendor**; it has been given to me, and I can give it* *to anyone I want to. If you worship me, it will all be yours."*

—Luke 4:5–7 (NIV)

As you know, Satan deceived Adam and Eve out of their authority and splendor. Again, our definition of plunder: something taken by force, **theft, or fraud**, often referring to the spoils of war or conquest.

In a nutshell, Satan has taken control of the money (splendor) and authority (the political system) of the kingdoms of the world, essentially the nations.

This is Satan's plunder—money and the political system— his most prized possessions. He controls it and hides behind it. But his kingdom has fallen, so why are these two areas for the most part still in the hands of Satan?

Because someone needs to go after it!

Satan discourages such a mission, especially in the church, to those who have the actual authority to go after it. But in the world, it is celebrated.

Satan fights and does his best to hide behind his lies which the Bible calls doctrines of devils! For example: it is wrong to have money; you are greedy if you have money; and churches should teach people to embrace vows of poverty, to name just a few. If you knock out the church, then only the world, those under his control, will gain wealth and authority and end up having total influence, as we have seen in the last few years here in the United States. Money plays a huge role in the political system—no let me rephrase that: money plays a huge role in every part of life where influence is needed.

Secondly, besides the wealth of the nations, Satan was given the authority of the nations. That is the political system. Think about what people say:

Never talk about politics and money in the church.

Are you kidding?

That is what Satan does not want you to talk about because both are about influence against his kingdom, but at the same time, are used to support the influence of his kingdom.

To actually plunder his kingdom, we need to infiltrate it with people who understand the authority that they walk in from God's perspective. We need to plunder his kingdom through people that build successful businesses and create the wealth needed to counter Satan's influence. When Israel came out of Egypt, they were barely a nation. Although they were spiritually, they were not physically. They had no land or borders and had yet to occupy the land God was giving them. But, in Deuteronomy, God gave them this promise:

*The Lord **will establish you** as his holy
people, as he promised you on oath, if you keep
the commands of the Lord your God and walk in
obedience to him. Then all the peoples on earth **will
see that you are called by the name of the Lord,
and they will fear you. The Lord will grant you
abundant prosperity**—in the fruit of your womb,
the young of your livestock and the crops of your
ground—in the land he swore to your ancestors to
give you.*

*The Lord will open the heavens, the storehouse of
his bounty, to send rain on your land in season and
to bless all the work of your hands. **You will lend
to many nations but will borrow from none.
The Lord will make you the head, not the tail.** If
you pay attention to the commands of the Lord your
God that I give you this day and carefully
follow them, you will always be at the top, never at
the bottom.*

—Deuteronomy 28:9–13 (NIV)

In verse 9, God says that they yet had to be established. Think of a tree taking root; it becomes permanently planted in the ground once the root system has spread out and dug deep.

*Then all the peoples on earth **will see that you
are called by the name of the Lord**, and they*

> *will fear you. The Lord will grant you abundant*
> *prosperity—in the fruit of your womb, the young of*
> *your livestock and the crops of your ground—in the*
> *land he swore to your ancestors to give you.*
> —Deuteronomy 28:10–11 (NIV)

What did they see? **Why did they fear them**? Because they had abundant prosperity. They had options. Because they were a wealthy nation, they would have the upper hand in trade and war.

> *You will lend to many nations but will borrow from*
> *none. The Lord will make you the head, not the tail.*
> —Deuteronomy 28:12b–13a (NIV)

You can only be the head if you control the money and the authority. Notice God says that you will lend before He says you will be the head. That is how it is. That is what Satan is fighting for: the money.

There is an old saying that says "follow the money." Let's be honest, there is no authority without money. Yes, you could have a military-based government ruling through fear, but do not be deceived. At the top, it is the bribes, the stolen UN shipments then sold on the black market, the state-owned drug deals, etc. There is a lot of money at the top of these corrupt governments.

Only the church has the anointing to root out demons and

dispel the lies of the enemy. But for those that will stand against the enemy and embrace the mission to go after Satan's plunder, there is reward.

> *Even now the one who reaps draws a wage and harvests a crop for eternal life, so that the sower and the reaper may be glad together.*
> —John 4:36 (NIV)

We are called and anointed to deal with demons!

No, we are not called to hide, but instead, we are on the largest plunder mission of all time! God wants His people back! But our mission is also to release the wealth that belongs to the church, enabling it to accomplish its mission, and also to free the financial inheritance that belongs to God's people. But for many in the church, they have no concept of what we are talking about.

I am sure that you have heard the story of Jericho and the walls that came tumbling down, as the children's song goes. But there is so much more to that story than the walls that came crashing down. Jericho was the first city that Joshua approached when Israel crossed the Jordan River into the Promised Land.

> *Now the gates of Jericho were securely barred because of the Israelites. No one went out and no one came in.*

Then the Lord said to Joshua, "See, I have delivered Jericho into your hands, along with its king [the authority] and its fighting men. March around the city once with all the armed men. Do this for six days. Have seven priests carry trumpets of rams' horns in front of the ark. On the seventh day, march around the city seven times, with the priests blowing the trumpets. When you hear them sound a long blast on the trumpets, have the whole army give a loud shout; then the wall of the city will collapse and the army will go up, everyone straight in."

—Joshua 6:1–5 (NIV)

I think we have all heard this story for years, and especially as children. But everyone talks about the walls coming down, but never about why the walls came down. Israel took the city and destroyed it. But they also plundered it, taking the gold and the silver into the Lord's own treasury. This money was set apart as holy to the Lord, as a tithe.

But I believe this story is also prophetic in a couple of ways. One, the walls coming down would be prophetic of Satan's walls coming down; his protection suddenly falling apart. Second, the loss of the king represents Satan's loss of authority over the city and his hidden treasures. And the fighting men? Satan's demons having now lost their legal ability to protect the plunder that the city held.

Once the walls came down, God's people were anointed to

go in and take the city and bring out the plunder that was there. Well, I have good news! Satan's walls are down, and Jesus gave us complete and absolute authority over Satan and his demons. His kingdom is now open to be plundered. What Satan claimed was his is now open and bare! You are empowered; now, go! The problem is that the church wants to sing and talk about the walls coming down but never about what is hidden behind those walls. Satan does not want you to find out about that treasure. He wants to intimidate you into thinking that his walls are still up, and he still has authority. But he is a liar.

I believe that God is showing me that this is a new season, a season of great harvest and plunder for the church. It will be a season of new methods, new direction and God-breathed plans. I would encourage you to lift your expectations, as I believe that God wants to do something so big that it astonishes people. That is what I keep getting in my spirit; there are huge harvests coming to those who hear His voice in this season. Even now, God is discerning who He can trust with what He wants to do. Here is an example of what will be happening.

> *You will still be eating last year's harvest when you*
> *will have to move it out to make room for the new.*
> —Leviticus 26:10 (NIV)

Do you remember the story of Jesus feeding the 5,000? Five loaves and two fish fed 10,000 to 20,000 people. The

Bible says there were 5,000 men there. If you add women and children, the total could have been as high as 20,000.

After Jesus multiplied the loaves and fish, the Bible says there were twelve baskets left over. That is truly a great picture of the double portion. But what I want to show you is how those twelve baskets of bread and fish came about. Of course, the Bible tells us that the disciples picked up the fragments that were left over, but they did not see that outcome at first.

> *When they had all had enough to eat, he said to his disciples, "Gather the pieces that are left over. **Let nothing be wasted.**"*
> —John 6:12 (NIV)

Let's put this statement in perspective. These disciples were untrained to discern what was really in front of their eyes. Jesus had to tell them, "Let nothing be wasted; pick up the fragments." He was still training them to see things differently.

Do you think that God is going to send them a huge gathering assignment before they learn how to discern what is in front of them? I mean, they were basically walking on top of these fragments without discerning what they were doing. Only Jesus was able to discern what was going on and to point out their lack of spiritual vision.

Let's look at another example of what I am saying. Look at 2 Kings chapter 4, a famous story for sure, but a sad one as well.

The wife of a man from the company of the prophets cried out to Elisha, "Your servant my husband is dead, and you know that he revered the Lord. But now his creditor is coming to take my two boys as his slaves."

Elisha replied to her, "How can I help you? Tell me, what do you have in your house?"

"Your servant has nothing there at all," she said, "except a small jar of olive oil."

Elisha said, "Go around and ask all your neighbors for empty jars. Don't ask for just a few. Then go inside and shut the door behind you and your sons. Pour oil into all the jars, and as each is filled, put it to one side."

She left him and shut the door behind her and her sons. They brought the jars to her and she kept pouring. When all the jars were full, she said to her son, "Bring me another one."

But he replied, "There is not a jar left." Then the oil stopped flowing.

She went and told the man of God, and he said,
"Go, sell the oil and pay your debts. You and your
sons can live on what is left."

—2 Kings 4:1–7 (NIV)

This woman was told that her answer was that God was going to multiply the oil, which she could sell to pay off her husband's debt and free her sons from forced labor to pay it off.

Elisha said, "Go around and ask all your neighbors
*for empty jars. **Don't ask for just a few.** Then go*
inside and shut the door behind you and your sons.
Pour oil into all the jars, and as each is filled, put
it to one side."

She left him and shut the door behind her and her
sons. They brought the jars to her and she kept
pouring. When all the jars were full, she said to her
*son, **"Bring me another one." But he replied,***
"There is not a jar left." <u>Then the oil stopped</u>
<u>flowing.</u>

—2 Kings 4:3–6 (NIV)

Of course, this is a great story of deliverance, and she was able to buy her sons out of slavery. But she missed it. I know you are shocked that I said that, aren't you? So, let me ask you, "When did the oil stop running?" When she ran out of jars. Do you not see it? God gave her the keys to an oil well and she controlled the flow. She could have gathered thousands of pots, and that oil would have just kept on flowing.

That is a great story. But why didn't Elisha just go to the treasury and pay her enough money to pay her two sons out of slavery? Her husband worked for the prophet. I believe the reason is because Elisha did not have enough to do what God wanted to do. God did not want to just pay off the debt, He wanted to really bless her and reward her for all the work and loyalty she and her husband had given Him.

Again, let me ask the question: do you think God is going to give someone an assignment that is bigger than they can spiritually discern? We should all pray that we can see what Elisha saw. The woman was consumed with getting enough money to pay her sons out of slavery, and she never saw what God was trying to give her.

I am telling you, pray that you can see what Elisha saw. There are some GREAT harvests coming and there is great plunder being freed up from Satan's hidden treasures in this season. Be prepared to listen to the Spirit in these days, so you can hear and not miss God's leading and timing.

I was amazed as Jacob told me his story a few months ago.

When Jacob was 16, he said he really did not want to get

a job, so he began to think of other ways to make money. COVID hit, and he could not go anywhere, so he thought he would try Internet marketing. Two and a half years went by and he said that he did not really make any money from the business and found himself living off credit cards, opening a new credit card as each card reached its limit.

Eventually, he had to get loans to pay off the credit cards in order to keep using them. He said it was a vicious cycle. He rang up over $70,000 in credit-card debt trying to survive. He was living at home with his parents who thought he was doing really well with his business. But he tried to hide the real facts from them, that things were not going that well.

In desperation, he looked to New Age teaching, where he thought he would find the reason why he was failing. After about six months, he came to a dead-end again and began to look into Jesus and being a Christian. He said that he immediately had a peace that let him know that God was real, and Jesus was his answer.

So, he began to study and soon came across our teaching of the Kingdom. He said he studied my books nonstop because he felt he had found his answer. When he came to my instruction on how to sow and reap, he said he spent some time studying that and comparing what I was saying with the Word until he became convinced that this principle was from God.

On November 13, 2023, he said he sowed his first seed. Three weeks later, he discovered a new product that he felt he could sell online. It was December 1 when he launched this new online business. The first day he said he made $2,000, but by the second week he had made $70,000 and paid his credit cards off. Now a year later, the business has brought in **six million dollars.** He gives all the credit to God and the Kingdom principles that he has learned.

Now that kind of harvest catches people attention, and Jacob has gone on to prosper at even greater levels since then.

Jacob is not an exception. I think the biggest advantage he had was knowing nothing about Christianity when he found my materials on the Kingdom. What I mean by that is that he did not have to unlearn a lot of religious teaching before he learned the truth, which is one reason why I believe he had such sudden success.

Some people say that money is not important, but it takes money to get things done on the earth. God is in the people business, and He is counting on us to gather the plunder that Satan has stolen. Satan is deceiving and holding people behind a wall of deception, and only you and I, who have the anointing of God, can get in there and bring them out.

If God sent His only son Jesus to pay our ransom, to free us from the kingdom of darkness, should we not join the team to help Him gather the plunder that Satan is sitting on? You may say, "Well, what is in it for me?" Well, of course, you would owe Jesus your life, and would be full of gratitude for what He has done for you. But let me tell you how good our God is.

Looking back at the story of Jericho, you might remember that all the treasure that was in Jericho was to be devoted to the Lord and go into the Lord's treasury as a tithe to the Lord. But when they went from Jericho, the Bible says this:

> You shall do to Ai and its king as you did to Jericho
> and its king, except that you may carry off their
> plunder and livestock for yourselves.
> —Joshua 8:2a (NIV)

After the tithe was paid at Jericho, everything they gathered from that point on was theirs to keep.

Helping God gather the plunder is not a hard, unrewarding task. No, God is good and not a hard taskmaster. He is generous and fair, and He will reward you.

When we first began to design the Now Center, we were a church of around 350. Our plan was to build up some cash and borrow some as well. We had outgrown the radio station that allowed us to use one of their rooms free of charge to launch our new church.

We had bought and paid for 22 acres and knew that it was

a good time to consider building a place of our own. We had plans drawn up, and when we got our first estimate to build the design, I remember sitting there with the banker. She said it would cost $4.7 million to build, not counting everything we had to put in the building and landscaping outside the building. I was shocked at the price. I was even more shocked when she said the payment would be $34,000 a month.

As I said, we were not planning to borrow all the money and were relying on cash to help bring the loan amount and the payment down. We asked each family to take some time to pray about it, and then in one service, we were going to ask them what they were willing to give to the project. Drenda and I at the time had around $50,000 in the bank but we also knew enough about the Kingdom of God that we knew God would bring more to us as we sowed.

So, I was thinking about giving $150,000. I mean, I had never in my life had that kind of money in my hands at one time before. But Drenda wanted to sow $200,000, which was really hard for me to believe for.

On the night of the meeting, my cousin's husband, who farmed hundreds of acres, attended. So Drenda asked him, "Dan, how much do you spend sowing your crops in a typical year?" He said, "Around $200,000." Well, that was confirmation. We said we would give $200,000, and the program we were using was saying that the families had a couple years to send that money in.

Now, the first thing we did after we said we would pay the $200,000 was to pray for the plan. Where should we look for the harvest on our initial $50,000 we had sown at the meeting? To answer that question, I need to let you know about a business opportunity that I had at the time. I own a company that works in the financial field. We use different vendors for different clients as their needs demand. One vendor that we had used for years has a once-a-year meeting where they celebrate the previous year's performance and recognize the top producers.

At the time, our main vendor had a bonus program based on production. But because I held an older contract with them, I was not eligible for that bonus. Well, that bothered me, so the next year I asked them about the bonus, and they repeated the same thing, that my company did not qualify for the bonus.

After we sowed that seed, I felt like the Lord was saying to call that company back about that bonus. I thought I already knew what they would say about that since I had just asked them a few months before this. I knew the last time I talked to the company, the gatekeeper would not let me talk to the vice president, who was the person who originally told me that I did not qualify. I had her email address, so I thought I would send an email, hoping that it would go straight to her. I was pleased that, in a week's time, I received from her an email saying, after giving the situation much thought, they had decided to give me the bonus.

The bonus that year was $200,000! Amazing, right? But that is not the best part of the story. To pay me the bonus, the company had to change my contract, which allowed me to participate in the bonus program every year since then. The conversation I had with the vice president about that bonus program happened many years ago, maybe twenty years or so. But, you know what? I have received that bonus every year since. That little change to my contract which enabled me to get that bonus paid out a bonus of $758,000 in 2025. How much did it pay me to pay that first $200,000 into our new building? The answer: nothing. And it has paid me millions over the years.

I hope that I have inspired you now to not only think in terms of having great harvests, but also to get involved in plundering the kingdom of hell. And the greatest treasure is a person's soul.

CHAPTER 6
PLUNDERING THE ENEMY'S CAMP

I want to start this chapter with a story that can help us understand how to go about the process of plundering. Sorry for the long text, but I believe we need to read this story all the way through.

> David and his men reached Ziklag on the third day. Now the Amalekites had raided the Negev and Ziklag. They had attacked Ziklag and burned it, and had taken captive the women and everyone else in it, both young and old. They killed none of them, but carried them off as they went on their way.
>
> When David and his men reached Ziklag, they found it destroyed by fire and their wives and sons and daughters taken captive. So David and his men wept aloud until they had no strength left to weep. David's two wives had been captured—Ahinoam of Jezreel and Abigail, the widow of Nabal of Carmel. David was greatly distressed because the men were

talking of stoning him; each one was bitter in spirit because of his sons and daughters. But David found strength in the Lord his God.

Then David said to Abiathar the priest, the son of Ahimelek, "Bring me the ephod." Abiathar brought it to him, and David inquired of the Lord, "Shall I pursue this raiding party? Will I overtake them?"

"Pursue them," he answered. "You will certainly overtake them and succeed in the rescue."

David and the six hundred men with him came to the Besor Valley, where some stayed behind. Two hundred of them were too exhausted to cross the valley, but David and the other four hundred continued the pursuit.

They found an Egyptian in a field and brought him to David. They gave him water to drink and food to eat—part of a cake of pressed figs and two cakes of raisins. He ate and was revived, for he had not eaten any food or drunk any water for three days and three nights.

David asked him, "Who do you belong to? Where do you come from?"

He said, "I am an Egyptian, the slave of an

Amalekite. My master abandoned me when I became ill three days ago. We raided the Negev of the Kerethites, some territory belonging to Judah and the Negev of Caleb. And we burned Ziklag." David asked him, "Can you lead me down to this raiding party?"

He answered, "Swear to me before God that you will not kill me or hand me over to my master, and I will take you down to them."

He led David down, and there they were, scattered over the countryside, eating, drinking and reveling because of the great amount of plunder they had taken from the land of the Philistines and from Judah. David fought them from dusk until the evening of the next day, and none of them got away, except four hundred young men who rode off on camels and fled. David recovered everything the Amalekites had taken, including his two wives. Nothing was missing: young or old, boy or girl, plunder or anything else they had taken. David brought everything back. He took all the flocks and herds, and his men drove them ahead of the other livestock, saying, "This is David's plunder."

—1 Samuel 30:1–20 (NIV)

Here we see that the enemy has taken David's family, his men's families, and everything of value in the camp.

The enemy had taken everything! This is where so many Christians stop and mourn their loses, but instead of advancing against the enemy to recover what was stolen, they embrace the lies of the enemy. Well, God knows best. It was His will. He is teaching me something through this.

NO! STOP IT. There is a thief who is wanting to take everything you have, and if that is not enough, he wants you to blame God for the loss. But in this story, there was a man of God who was not going to allow this to be the final story that would be told. David took a moment to regain his composure over the event that he was facing and then the Bible says, *"But David found strength in the Lord his God."*

I am sure this means that David was remembering the victories that God had already brought him through. I am sure his victory over Goliath was a victory he was remembering, or maybe his more recent victory that he had at Keilah, fighting the Philistines (1 Samuel 23). After he found courage in the Lord, he prayed to hear God's instruction regarding what to do. Should he go after his family, his men's families, and their things? The Lord said, yes.

Step One: Know God is for you and meditate on past victories to strengthen yourself in the Lord.

Step one in taking back something the enemy has plundered is to realize that this is the enemy, and not God's will. Your life is holy ground, and the enemy cannot touch you or your possessions, unless you have sinned and opened the door to destruction or allowed your words to become perverted, where you come into agreement with fear, and you have opened the door and given the enemy jurisdiction. In that case, you will need to shut the door and align your thoughts and your words with what God says about you and the situation.

For instance, if you always say, "I get a cold every winter," then do not be surprised if you get sick every winter. If you have sinned, then simply repent, acknowledge your error and get back up on your feet and do what David did: pray, and ask the Lord for direction, which is step two.

Step Two: Inquire of the Lord how to proceed.

Several years ago, when we lived in Tulsa, my uncle came out to visit us. It was a great visit, and he was gracious enough to help us remodel our bathroom. He had driven his RV, and the night he was leaving, I came home after being at an appointment. Seeing him getting into his RV, I went to say goodbye to him.

I talked for a little while with him and I remember setting my car keys down in his RV. I forgot about the keys until after he left, and this was the in the days before cell phones. This was the only set of keys we had for the car and church was the next day. I was concerned because Drenda and I were involved with the church and the Sunday morning service.

We prayed for those keys to be returned; that my uncle or aunt would see them before they got too far away and bring them back, but that did not happen.

Sunday morning, we got up and we thought about asking a friend to pick us up, or we could try the old car we had that did not start most of the time and was unsafe. While I was getting dressed, I reached into the back of my closet and grabbed my dress shoes. As I was putting my foot into the shoe, I felt something hard up in the toe of the shoe. When I turned the shoe over, the car keys fell out onto the floor. I stood there stunned. How did they get in there? I had left them in my uncle's RV. The only explanation is that an angel retrieved them for us and put them in that shoe to be sure that I would find them that morning. There is no other explanation possible.

Learn not to react to every situation out of a knee-jerk response. Take the time to reflect on the Lord, and then pray for direction and the plan to regain what was lost.

Through the deer hunting lessons that God has given me over the years, I have learned to never give up on my faith. When Drenda and I built our beautiful home in the country, I was thrilled that it was filled with woods and deer. I would go out after sowing my seed, as I mentioned earlier in this book, and would bring back my buck. But I always thought how great it would be if I could harvest a really big trophy buck from my own property for my office wall. I was getting nice bucks every year, but nothing that I would say was worthy of mounting.

One day, Drenda reminded me about my desire for a big buck for the office and encouraged me to sow a seed for a trophy buck for the upcoming hunting season. I had a hard time with that. I had been hunting the property for the last five years, and I had never seen a trophy-sized deer out there. In fact, I felt I did not have faith for such a deer, and I knew I could not sow a seed for one if it was not in faith.

So, I sowed for the normal four-point or bigger buck, which I knew would be great eating. I realized that I needed to pray more about that trophy buck before I could sow a seed in faith. The night before I was to go hunting, as Drenda and I prayed over the next morning, I told her that I just did not have faith for the trophy buck that year. She then stopped me and said, "You have faith for the deer, and I will have faith for the trophy buck."

As I sat in my tree stand that morning, sure enough, in about twenty minutes, a nice four-point shows up. I was hunting with my crossbow, and as I pulled the trigger, the buck took a step, and my arrow hit the buck high. It was not a good shot and I waited in the tree for a bit before I began to track him.

As I got out of the tree, I found blood on my arrow and a decent blood trail out of the woods into the cornfield behind my woods. I thought I possibly hit a blood vessel, and the deer might yet be harvested. I slowly tracked the buck for about a half hour until I lost the trail. The blood trail had been getting smaller and smaller for a while, and now it had vanished.

I knew my shot was not a sure kill shot and thought maybe the deer would live, but I was upset with myself for missing the shot and was tempted to go back to the house and call it a day. At this point I was out in the middle of the cornfield where a small ravine weaved itself through the corn.

As I stood there for a moment thinking about my missed opportunity, I remembered other days when I thought all was lost and how God brought a second chance along. So, I prayed and reloaded my bow and slowly made my way along the ravine toward home.

Suddenly, as I was slowly moving along, a deer jumped up out of the ravine and ran into the cornfield and stopped directly in front of me about 55 yards out. I was wearing camo and the deer had stopped to see what I was. I could see that the deer was a nice buck and had a nice rack with drop tines.

It all happened so fast that I did not have time to really get a good look at the antlers. I knew the buck would bolt at any second. The shot was a guess; I had never shot at a deer at that distance before, but I aimed just a little over his back and let the arrow go. In shock, I saw the buck drop to the ground.

As I walked up to the buck, I saw that it was huge! It had 26 points on its rack, and yes, it had drop tines. The buck qualified for the Buckeye Big Buck Club in Ohio and its rack scored 177 points by the Boone and Crockett

REMEMBER, IT IS NEVER TOO LATE FOR GOD TO RESTORE WHAT YOU THINK IS LOST.

scoring standards. And yes, it is on the wall in my office today, and it still the biggest buck I have ever shot.

It was only because of my previous experience with God that I knew not to throw in the towel after I had lost the trail of the four-point buck. Actually, if I had not shot at the four-point, I would have never had the shot at the 26-point buck. It was the four-point buck that led me to where the big buck was bedded down. Remember, it is never too late for God to restore what you think is lost.

Step Three: Follow the Lord's leading and engage the plan.

Notice in David's plan to recapture his family that he did not know where the enemy's camp was, but God had said, "Yes, go after your family, all will be saved." David and his men left with confidence that all was not lost yet did not really know where the enemy's camp was.

This left them at a huge disadvantage. By just stumbling forward they could have easily been seen by the enemy in which the enemy would attack them or run before they could engage them. Surprise would be David's greatest advantage, but that was something he did not have when he started out. But God was there leading all the way.

You and I may not know how or where to look to recapture what the enemy has stolen, but God does. He will lead you just as David stumbled upon that Egyptian who was half starved and who knew exactly where the enemy camp was so that he could lead them to that camp, giving David the advantage of surprise.

Step 4 (similar to step three): Engage the plan and be relentless.

> *David fought them from dusk until the evening of the next day, and none of them got away, except four hundred young men who rode off on camels and fled.*
>
> —1 Samuel 30:17 (NIV)

David engaged the battle at dusk and fought them all night long and until the evening of the next day. That is being relentless. They were already very tired, and 200 men said they were too tired to continue and had stayed behind. The ones who engaged the battle were tired also, but they stayed engaged until all was recovered.

Step 5: It is not just about your stuff.

> *David recovered everything the Amalekites had taken, including his two wives.* **Nothing was missing***: young or old, boy or girl, plunder or anything else they had taken. David brought everything back. He took all the flocks and herds, and* **his men drove them ahead of the other livestock, saying, "This is David's plunder."**
>
> —1 Samuel 30:18–20 (NIV)

This raiding party had been raiding other areas before they came to Ziklag. Yes, David recovered all his stuff and his people, yet we see his men leading "other livestock," besides what was taken from Ziklag. This is the plunder that this raiding party had stolen from other cities before they came to Ziklag. God will lead you into situations where you will be recovering plunder that you yourself have not lost. God wants it back! That is His plunder. Always be open and aware of that.

As an example, I was visiting with some pastors at a conference one day, and they were telling me about a rebate program that I had not heard about. I really had not wanted to go to that conference but decided to go at the last minute. I looked into this rebate program and found it to be valid. So, we applied for it. Over a year went by and we heard nothing from them. As all churches go through up and down fluctuations with their cash flow, we found ourselves in a lower cash balance than I felt comfortable with, when suddenly this check for almost $900,000 shows up. Guess where that came from? That rebate program that I knew nothing about. That money was not money I had lost; that was money that God knew about and wanted us to grab. We had submitted that rebate over a year and a half before, but it showed up right on time. God wanted me at that conference; He knew that we would need that check when it arrived.

We must always be open to the fragments that God is pointing out to us. Just like the disciples were walking on the fragments, not realizing what they were doing. God does not want anything to be wasted; He has plans for it.

Remember, God is going to lead people He can trust into great and awesome opportunities in this season. Great harvests are coming to God's people in this season! Recovery and restoration of what has been lost will be happening in this season. So, the next time you think of having great harvests, do not forget the plunder that may be right in front of you. Ask God to show it to you!

Drenda and I have owned a company that helps people get out of debt for 33 years and counting. We specialize in showing people that they can be debt free in less than seven years, including their mortgage, without changing their income. This company was birthed by a dream one night when we were crying out for direction. We were just learning how the Kingdom worked, and we knew God was going to show us the direction to take, which He did.

Showing people how to get out of debt as a business was a shocker to me since we were the poster children of what never to do with a credit card. I thought possibly God was wrong about that idea, however, by faith we launched that company, and it has been extremely successful all these years.

But the company has changed over the years. God would point things out to us, things He wanted us to capture. In 2001, He showed me that He wanted me to grab a new product that was just coming out on the market which would protect a client's investment from downturns in the market yet capture the upswing permanently, without charging up-front broker fees or annual fees. It was a hit. Little did I know at that time that these products would help save my clients, God's people, thousands upon thousands of dollars in potential losses over the years.

One of our primary jobs at Forward Financial Group is to look for ways we can lower costs, to free up money for debt reduction. One of those areas we look at is their current debt structure. Many times, we can find drastic savings here by consolidating high-interest rate credit card debt into a line of credit or fixed rate against their home's equity.

For years, I would tell our clients to go to their own bank and put that structure in place. But one day the Lord said to me,

"Why are you doing that?" I was confused. As I stopped and prayed about what He had said, I knew the answer. He was asking me why I was sending these people down the road to their bank to do this. I was the one that was identifying the savings and the method. Why would I not capture the profit on my advice? I am already sitting down with my client to cover all the numbers on such a transaction.

Of course, I knew instantly why I had not considered starting my own mortgage company. Training, licensing, plus a full-time person is required by state law, and I thought I really did not have time to do that. But again, I felt the Lord prompting me to reconsider, which I did. And I successfully launched our own mortgage company, and that first year made a net profit of $166,000. That is $166,000 that was always there but not being picked up.

There were many areas like that God would show me. I guess you could say that fragment was right there the whole time, and like the disciples, I was walking around it but not seeing what was there. Maybe you are doing the same? Stop and think about it. Pray about it. God will show you things you have never seen before but were there all along.

I want to leave you with this section of Isaiah 61. The entire chapter is telling us the benefits of the Year of the Jubilee and vengeance (plunder). These benefits are yours now! But I like this part of the chapter; it is talking about you! Be encouraged.

You will feed on the wealth of nations,
*   and in their riches you will boast.*
Instead of your shame
*   you will receive a double portion,*
and instead of disgrace
*   you will rejoice in your inheritance.*
And so you will inherit a double portion in your land,
*   and everlasting joy will be yours.*
"For I, the Lord, love justice;
*   I hate robbery and wrongdoing.*
In my faithfulness I will reward my people
*   and make an everlasting covenant with them.*
Their descendants will be known among the nations
*   and their offspring among the peoples.*
All who see them will acknowledge
*   that they are a people the Lord has blessed."*
                                    —Isaiah 61:6b–9 (NIV)

BIBLIOGRAPHY

Chapter 1

[1] "Everything You Need to Know About Stress," posted November 20, 2023, Mass General Brigham McLean, https://www.mcleanhospital.org/essential/stress.

[2] "Everything You Need to Know About Stress."

[3] "Everything You Need to Know About Stress."

[4] "Everything You Need to Know About Stress."

[5] "Stress: Statistics," Mental Health Foundation, https://www.mentalhealth.org.uk/explore-mental-health/statistics/stress-statistics.

[6] "Stress Fact Sheet 2020," Mental Health Association of Maryland, https://www.mhamd.org/wp-content/uploads/2019/10/Stress-Fact-Sheet-2020.pdf.

[7] Batdorf, Emily, "Living Paycheck to Paycheck Statistics 2024," posted April 2, 2024, *Forbes*, https://www.forbes.com/advisor/banking/living-paycheck-to-paycheck-statistics-2024/.

[8] Sturt, David, and Todd Nordstrom, "10 Shocking Workplace Stats You Need To Know," Posted March 8, 2018, *Forbes*, https://www.forbes.com/sites/davidsturt/2018/03/08/10-shocking-workplace-stats-you-need-to-know/?sh=3130ab42f3af.

ABOUT THE AUTHOR

Gary Keesee is a television host, author, international speaker, financial expert, successful entrepreneur, and pastor who has made it his mission to help people win in life, especially in the areas of faith, family, and finances.

After years of living in poverty, Gary and his wife, Drenda, discovered the principles of the Kingdom of God, and their lives were drastically changed. Together, under the direction of the Holy Spirit, they created several successful businesses and paid off all of their debt. Now, they spend their time declaring the Good News of the Kingdom of God around the world through Faith Life Now, their organization that exists to motivate, educate, and inspire people from all walks of life and backgrounds to pursue success, walk out their God-designed purposes, and leave positive spiritual and moral legacies for their families.

Faith Life Now produces two television programs—*Fixing the Money Thing* and *Drenda*—as well as practical resources, conferences, and speaking events around the world.

Gary is also the president and founder of Forward Financial Group and the founding pastor of Faith Life Church, which has campuses in Central Ohio.

Gary and Drenda, their five adult children and their spouses, and their grandchildren all reside in Central Ohio.

For additional resources by both Gary and Drenda, visit FaithLifeNow.com.

FINANCIAL REVOLUTION CONFERENCES

If you're a pastor or leader in your church, you probably have plenty of vision for your ministry. But do you have the money or resources you need to support the vision?

If your church is like most churches, the answer is probably *not quite* or even *no*.

Why?

We've found one of the biggest reasons is DEBT. So many Christians are being held *hostage* by debt.

Your people *WANT* to financially support the ministry and vision of your church, but many of them are living paycheck to paycheck with no hope of breaking free.

We can help.

For more than 25 years now, we've been working with churches of all sizes, helping them reach their goals and see their visions for their ministries become reality. And the best part is that this is completely free!

We help churches by helping their people. We can help *your church* by helping *your people*.

Learn more at **ftmtevent.com.**

YOUR FINANCIAL REVOLUTION
5-BOOK PAPERBACK BOXED SET

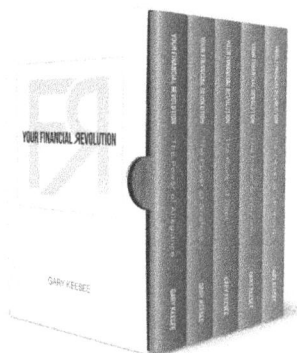

Gary Keesee went from being completely desperate financially and physically to healthy and whole, paying cash for cars, building his home free from debt, starting multiple companies, and teaching hundreds of thousands of people about Kingdom living each week through television, ministry, and books just like these.

What changed for Gary, and how can it change YOUR LIFE?

Scan to order your copy. →

Your answers are in the pages of THIS book series.

This isn't just another set of books with tips on how to fix your finances.

Full of fresh revelation, powerful examples from the Word of God, and inspiring personal stories about Gary and others who applied the foundational teachings from these five Kingdom principles in their own lives and experienced drastic change as a result, this series of books was written to help YOU experience real change in EVERY area of your life.

No matter your situation, there are answers. It's never too late.

You can have your own amazing story!

Join Gary Keesee on this incredible five-part journey of discovery that will completely revolutionize YOUR life… just like it did his.

This set contains paperback versions of Gary's complete *Your Financial Revolution* book series:

- *Your Financial Revolution: The Power of Allegiance*
- *Your Financial Revolution: The Power of Rest*
- *Your Financial Revolution: The Power of Strategy*
- *Your Financial Revolution: The Power of Provision*
- *Your Financial Revolution: The Power of Generosity*

Get your copy of the complete *Your Financial Revolution* five-book series at garykeesee.com.

You can also give at garykeesee.netviewshop.com/donate.

www.ingramcontent.com/pod-product-compliance
Lightning Source LLC
Chambersburg PA
CBHW070449090426
42735CB00012B/2496